Lecture Notes in Computer Sci

T0259845

Commenced Publication in 1973
Founding and Former Series Editors:
Gerhard Goos, Juris Hartmanis, and Jan van Leeuwen

Editorial Board

Charlotte Magnusson   Delphine Szymczak
Stephen Brewster (Eds.)

Haptic and Audio
Interaction Design

7th International Conference, HAID 2012
Lund, Sweden, August 23-24, 2012
Proceedings

 Springer

Volume Editors

Charlotte Magnusson
Delphine Szymczak
Lund University, Department of Design Sciences
P.O. Box 118, 22100 Lund, Sweden
E-mail: {charlotte.magnusson, delphine.szymczak}@certec.lth.se

Stephen Brewster
University of Glasgow, School of Computing Science
Glasgow, G12 8QQ, UK
E-mail: stephen.brewster@glasgow.ac.uk

ISSN 0302-9743   e-ISSN 1611-3349
ISBN 978-3-642-32795-7   e-ISBN 978-3-642-32796-4
DOI 10.1007/978-3-642-32796-4
Springer Heidelberg Dordrecht London New York

Library of Congress Control Number: 2012944601

CR Subject Classification (1998): H.5.1-2, K.4, H.1.2, H.5.5, K.3.1

LNCS Sublibrary: SL 3 – Information Systems and Application, incl. Internet/Web
and HCI

Typesetting: Camera-ready by author, data conversion by Scientific Publishing Services, Chennai, India

Printed on acid-free paper

Springer is part of Springer Science+Business Media (www.springer.com)

Preface

The sense of touch, together with gestures and sounds – in fact all the nonvisual interaction channels – are as yet sadly undervalued and underused in most applications today. Yet these modalities are becoming increasingly important for good mobile user experiences. One can no longer just focus on the screen in the mobile use situation; the use is embedded in a context where people and events in the environment may need your attention. More nonvisual interaction designs will simply make applications and devices easier for everyone to use. HAID 2012, the 7th International Workshop on Haptic and Audio Interaction Design, brings together efforts in this challenging area. How do we design effectively for mobile interaction? How can we design effective haptic, audio, and multimodal interfaces? In what new application areas can we apply these techniques? Are there design methods that are useful? Or evaluation techniques that are particularly appropriate?

In these proceedings you will find papers on how navigation can be supported by the use of sounds, touch, and gestures, papers on how nonvisual modalities can create rewarding user experiences, work on how interaction, objects, and interfaces should be designed – but also reports from more detailed studies and research on how to properly evaluate these types of designs.

The importance of sounds, gestures, and touch in mobile settings is evident by the fact that HAID 2012 was organized in collaboration with HaptiMap. This EU project on haptic, audio, and visual interfaces for maps and location-based services is funded by the European Commission in its Seventh Framework Programme under the Cooperation Programme ICT – Information and Communication Technologies (Challenge 7 – Independent living and inclusion). More information about HaptiMap can be found at the project website: www.haptimap.org.

The papers in these proceedings reflect promising progress in the field of haptics and audio interaction, but also show that these types of interactions present challenges – and that much work remains to be done in the field. The day when it is taken for granted that haptics and audio are important and necessary components in all applications and devices is still distant – but HAID 2012 has taken us one step further toward achieving this goal.

August 2012   Charlotte Magnusson

Organization

The 7th International Workshop on Haptic and Audio Interaction Design was organized by Lund University (Sweden), Certec, Division of Rehabilitation Engineering Research in the Department of Design Sciences, Faculty of Engineering and the University of Glasgow (UK), Department of Computing Science.

Conference Chairs

Charlotte Magnusson   Lund University, Sweden
                           Certec, Rehabilitation Engineering Research
Kirsten Rassmus-Gröhn   Lund University, Sweden
                           Certec, Rehabilitation Engineering Research
Stephen Brewster   University of Glasgow, UK
                           Department of Computing Science

Program Committee

Helen Petrie   University of York, UK
David McGookin   University of Glasgow, UK
Ian Oakley   Universidade da Madeira, Portugal
Sile O'Modhrain   University of Michigan, USA
Eva-Lotta Sallnäs   Royal Institute of Technology, Sweden
Antti Pirhonen   University of Jyväskylä, Finland
Ercan Altinsoy   Dresden University of Technology, Germany
Wilko Heuten   OFFIS, Germany
Roope Raisamo   University of Tampere, Finland
Johan Kildal   NOKIA, Finland
Federico Fontana   University of Udine, Italy
Marcelo Wanderley   McGill University, Canada
Stefania Serafin   Aalborg University Copenhagen, Denmark
Ravi Kuber   UMBC, USA
Emanuel Habets   University of Erlangen-Nuremberg, Germany
Andrew Crossan   University of Glasgow, UK
Nicolas Castagne   ACROE, France
Antonio Frisoli   Scuola Superiore Sant'Anna, Italy
Yon Visell   UPMC Université Paris 06, France

Table of Contents

Test and Evaluation

Understanding Auditory Navigation
to Physical Landmarks

David McGookin and Stephen A. Brewster

School of Computing Science
University of Glasgow, Glasgow, G12 8QQ
{David.McGookin,Stephen.Brewster}@glasgow.ac.uk
http://www.dcs.gla.ac.uk/~mcgookdk

Abstract. We present two studies that seek to better understand the role spatialised (3D) audio can play in supporting effective pedestrian navigation. 24 participants attempted to navigate and locate physical landmarks in a local botanical gardens using a gpsTunes [1] based auditory navigation system coupled with a map. Participants were significantly better at locating prominent than non-prominent physical landmarks. However, no significant quantative difference was found between the use of a map only and map + audio. Qualitative analysis revealed significant issues when physical landmarks are used, and common strategies when combining audio and map navigation. We highlight the implications of these in relation to existing work, and provide guidelines for future designers to employ.

Keywords: 3D Audio, Pedestrian Navigation, Maps, Landmarks.

1 Introduction

The wide scale deployment of modern smartphones has lead to a renewed interest in the ways pedestrians navigate their environment. Research has shown such navigation to be much more diverse than the turn-by-turn navigation employed when driving [2]. This has lead to new ways to support users navigation of the environment. Whilst haptic, specifically tactile, feedback has been investigated (e.g. [3]), a much more established technique is to provide bearing and distance information to a user via spatialised audio presentation (3D sound). Users hear, through a set of headphones, a geo-fixed spatialised sound that emanates from a location in the environment. This auditory cue can then be used as a virtual landmark to navigate towards. Although over a decade old, with repeated studies showing it to be effective, there are still many aspects of this technique we do not understand. In this paper we outline some of these, why they are important and present two studies that seek to better understand their impact in auditory navigation.

2 Related Work

The use of 3D audio as a means of guiding users in the physical environment has been considered for around a decade. The AudioGPS system [4] aimed to

C. Magnusson, D. Szymczak, and S. Brewster (Eds.): HAID 2012, LNCS 7468, pp. 1–10, 2012.

provide a MAUI (Minimal Attention User Interface), and remove the necessity to look at GPS screens whilst navigating. Rather than full 3D audio via a head-related transfer function (HRTF), stereo panning was used to indicate direction. A Geiger counter metaphor, with custom designed auditory pulses that repeated more rapidly as the user approached a virtual landmark, was used to indicate distance. Holland, Morse and Gedenryd showed, in informal tests, that users could successfully pilot along a route of these virtual auditory landmarks [4]. Landmarks were presented one at a time. When the user came close enough (approximately 10m), the landmark was switched off and the next was presented. Other work has extended this principle, investigating different types of audio and adding inertial sensors, such as magnetometers (a digital compass), to obtain more accurate heading data.

Strachan, Eslambolchilar and Murray-Smith's [1] gpsTunes used panning of a playing music track, rather than a custom designed auditory cue, to indicate direction. Music volume was increased as the user approached the target. They found users were able to successfully pilot along a route of four virtual landmarks in an open grassy area. They noted that such navigation might be integrated with a map, and adapted for more exploratory navigation (such as proposed by Allen [2]). However, they carried out no work to investigate this. More recent work has shown the basic technique to hold when the environment is "cluttered" with environmental features users must navigate around [5], rather than being an open grass area, and that it is useful to indicate general areas, such as in navigating a zoo [6]. Work has also applied the technique to navigation for blind and visually impaired pedestrians [7].

However, there are still many gaps in our knowledge. Firstly, the previous work assumes that users are navigating towards "virtual" landmarks: there is no physical manifestation of a landmark or waypoint in the environment. Jones et al. [5] observed that users were often drawn toward physical objects that were close to virtual landmarks, although the objects only happened to be in the environment and played no part in their study. McGookin, Brewster and Priego [8] and Vazquez-Alvarez, Oakley and Brewster [9] did associate sounds with physical objects, but it was their system, rather than the user, that determined if the objects had been reached. This is unlike everyday navigation where a user is trying to uniquely identify a physical landmark [10].

Michon and Denis [11] note the importance of landmarks in both making decisions when navigating, and confirming that the correct path is being taken. They note that landmarks that are prominent (stand out from their surroundings) are more useful than those that blend in. However, the goal of users is often to find these non-prominent landmarks. In ethnographic studies of navigation by tourists, Brown and Chalmers [10] note that even with a map and guidebook it is often difficult for tourists to find a landmark if it is not prominent (such as a small statue), even when close by. They note the example of a group of tourists trying to locate a specific building along a street. The group required a prolonged discussion around a guidebook and map, as well as input from the investigators, to correctly identify the building. There is no guidance as to the usefulness of

Fig. 1. Examples of landmarks used in the studies. Left: a non-prominent named bush landmark (shown with context). Right: a prominent signpost landmark (shown with context).

pedestrian audio navigation when the audio is coupled to real, physical landmarks that a user is trying to locate. The user must know that he or she has reached the physical landmark. Simply being told that this has occurred (e.g. [5,6,9]), without the user being able to visually identify the landmark, is unlikely to be helpful. In addition, as users often employ multiple navigation aids [10], auditory navigation is unlikely to be used alone. Seager [12] notes that north-up maps (where the map does not auto rotate) are considerably harder to relate to the environment, but users often do not rotate them to make this alignment easier. Egocentric cues, such as the use of spatial audio, may assist this, but it is unclear how users would divide the task between multiple aids. Is it necessary for audio to be presented throughout the entire navigation process, or if not, when should audio be presented? It is unclear how auditory navigation will integrate with maps and other aids.

3   Study Outline

To investigate these issues two within groups studies were carried out. All participants were pre-screened on the perspective taking spatial orientation test developed by Kozhevnikov and Hegarty [13]. Participants had to complete the test within a 15 minute period to proceed with the study. Twelve different participants took part in each study (Study 1: 7 male, 5 female, mean age 24. Study 2: 6 male, 6 female, mean age 25.5). Participants were recruited via notices placed around campus. The majority of participants were students studying on a variety of courses. Each study contained 3 conditions described later. In each condition participants had to find and photograph 6 different landmarks. Three sets of 6 landmarks were selected in the Glasgow Botanic Gardens. Each set contained three prominent and three non-prominent landmarks. Each set was counterbalanced between conditions in each study. Based on the work of Caduff

Fig. 2. Screenshot of the map and visual interface used in the studies (left). Showing the gps location of the user (blue marker) and the name and location of the landmark (red marker). In addition to panning the map, the user could use the "Find Me" and "Find Landmark" buttons to automatically move the map to show either the current location or landmark. When the user though the landmark had been reached, the user tapped the "Photograph Point of Interest" button and took a photograph of it (right).

and Timpf [14], prominence was determined by how much the landmarks varied from their surroundings. Non-prominent landmarks tended to be trees or shrubs labelled with their species name (allowing them to be uniquely identified), whilst prominent landmarks tended to be signposts (see Fig. 1) or large signs.

Participants used a custom iPhone application (see Fig. 2) showing an Open-StreetMap (`www.openstreetmap.org`) map of the park. The map showed current user location, and the name and location of the landmark to find. The application also provided a spatialised auditory environment (using OpenAL) containing a single broadband auditory source (a bubbling water sound). This was presented through headphones (Sennheiser HD-25). The sound was geo-located at the position of the physical landmark. We used the same design as gpsTunes [1]: presenting directional audio that increased in volume as the user approached. We used the bubbling water sound to retain consistency between the conditions, though as noted by McGookin, Brewster and Priego [8], this sound could be replaced by any auditory source depending on the scenario of use. We used a high accuracy (<5m mean horizontal accuracy) external GPS unit (QStarz BT-Q1000XT) to determine position, and the internal magnetometer of the iPhone to determine orientation. On each trial participants navigated from a start location to the landmark (mean length 150-200m) using the map and audio as they felt appropriate. They were told to always take the shortest route and to remain on the park paths at all times. Cutting across the grass was not allowed. As soon as participants felt they had identified the landmark, irrespective of their distance from it, they photographed it using the iPhone, ending the trial. The location and distance from the landmark that the user took the photograph allowed us to determine at what point the navigation aid became redundant. In other words, the point at which the user's confidence that the landmark was the correct one meant that he or she no longer needed to be guided. Participants were then walked to the real landmark, which acted as the start location for the next trial. At the end of the study each participant was interviewed and debriefed on the experiment, their condition preference and strategies in completing the tasks.

How far the participant was from the physical landmark before the audio landmark was audible (audio distance) was the main factor and had three levels in each study. In Study 1 this was either 15m, 30m or 15m + GPS Accuracy[1]. In Study 2 this was either 30m, Always On (audio was played from the start of the trial) or Never On (no audio was presented, users could only use the map). These boundaries provided a good range to understand if, and when, audio was useful. Landmark prominence (2 levels - prominent, non-prominent) was treated as a second factor.

4   Quantative Results

For each trial, distance walked was converted to a proportion of the shortest possible path distance a participant could have walked between the start of the trial and landmark location (POD). Distance walked was measured using a pedometer worn by participants[2]. A baseline-measuring phase, with the user walking a 100m section of path 10 times, was carried out at the start of the study. This was used to calibrate the pedometer. Time taken was converted to a proportion of the optimal time (POT) that participant would have taken to walk the shortest path at his or her normal walking speed. Normal walking speed was determined in the same baseline-measuring phase as for POD using the technique of [15]. A summary of all quantative results is shown in Table 1.

Results were analysed for each study using two-way ANOVAs (audio distance and landmark prominence as levels). No significance was found on any measure for audio distance; irrespective of whether audio was presented or not. Landmark prominence showed significance on all measures (see Table 2). Participants were able to identify and photograph prominent landmarks from further away, and were able to identify them more accurately. No significant interaction was found between audio distance and landmark prominence.

---

[1] For 15m + GPS Accuracy the audio distance was dynamic, being at least 15m plus the transient horizontal accuracy measure of the GPS unit. Hence it grew with poor GPS accuracy and shrank as GPS accuracy improved.

[2] We trialed three measures to determine distance: GPS, pedometer and Gait Analysis. Of these, the pedometer was the most consistent across all participants in the baseline-measuring phase.

Table 1. Overview of quantative performance of prominent (p) and non-prominent (np) landmarks for both studies. A value < 100% for POT or POD indicates super-optimal performance. Performance would be super-optimal if the participant photographed the landmark from a distance.

Measure	Study 1						Study 2					
	15m		*15m+GPS*		*30m*		*30m*		*Always On*		*Never On*	
	p	np	p	np	p	np	p	np	p	np	p	np
Identification Accuracy (of 3)	3	2.58	3	2.75	2.9	2.8	3	2.25	3	2.58	2.92	2.33
Photo Distance (meters)	31.76	8.67	31	8.32	33.66	11.27	34.18	7.36	22.7	7.36	19.60	6.63
POD (% of optimal distance)	90	118	92	112	92	121	98	140	100	154	117	151
POT (% of optimal time)	119	168	118	152	115	171	127	231	139	228	140	205

Table 2. Overview of ANOVA results for landmark prominence

Measure	Study 1		Study 2	
	F(1,11)	*p*	*F(1,11)*	*p*
Identification Accuracy	4.56	0.050	19.96	<0.001
Photo Distance	71.67	<0.001	33.25	<0.001
POD	20.29	< 0.001	39.82	<0.001
POT	30.40	< 0.001	153.24	<0.001

5   Qualitative Results

Given the previous work discussed, it is surprising that audio appears to have had no impact on navigation performance. Performance was similar between all audio conditions and the visual condition (Never On), both for prominent and non-prominent landmarks. To understand why this was the case we coded post-experimental interview data and event logging files using a grounded theory approach [16]. Initial codes were based on how participants had split the task between the sound and map, and differences based on the condition and landmark types.

Overall, participants strongly favoured the 30m condition (9 participants in Study 1 and 12 in Study 2). This was primarily as it best fitted into a three-stage strategy all participants employed. They described how the map was initially useful to determine the route and start to navigate towards the landmark. As they grew closer, and started to hear the audio, the sound assisted in confirming the correct direction (playing a similar role to the intermediate visual landmarks of Michon and Denis [11]): *"At the start you have the visual (display) to see the target, then you have the audio to confirm when you are getting closer, or confirm you are going in the right direction"*. At this point participants primarily switched to the audio as their main navigation aid, combining this with visual

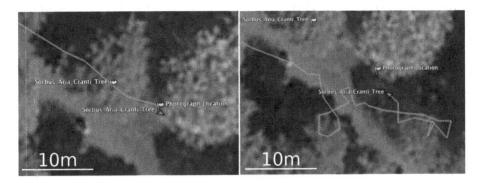

Fig. 3. Illustration of successful (left) and unsuccessful (right) audio use to home onto a non-prominent landmark

search of the environment to home onto the landmark: *"Most of the time I used the visual map, until at a really close distance, and then I used the audio to tell me left or right and then home in"*. Although there were minor variations in the strategy, the overall approach: map to navigate, audio to home and visual search to confirm, was common. Participants in Study 2, who completed the visual only condition, noted that the absence of audio made the task harder: *"no audio was more difficult. For times when I was looking, the audio was definitely helpful"*. In the 15m auditory distance condition participants felt the audio was presented too late, and in the Always On condition participants tended to "tune out" of the sound early on. This condition also lost the advantage of the audio indicating that the user was closing on the landmark: *"I liked the first one (30m condition) because the sound wasn't on all the time. So you could get close to the place and then it was good for directions you should go in"*.

The full execution of the three stage strategy was largely only seen in the search for non-prominent landmarks. For prominent landmarks, participant distance from the landmark when it was photographed (indicating the participant had found it) was around 32m for all conditions in Study 1, as well as the 30m condition for Study 2. For the visual (no audio) and always on conditions from Study 2, the photograph was taken approximately 20m from the landmark (these differences were not significant p=0.064). In the vast majority of trials participants had already determined the prominent landmark before hearing any audio, and thus it was mentioned to play little part. However, a small minority of participants mentioned that they had used the commencement of sound in the 30m condition as a confirmation that the prominent landmark was the correct one: *"I thought the signpost was the right one. I was about to take the photograph earlier, but I wasn't sure as I missed the previous one. I was getting closer and closer until I heard the audio. Then I was sure"*.

Given that participants were both positive towards audio, and clearly incorporated it into their strategies, its lack of impact supporting location of non-prominent landmarks is surprising. From our analysis it was the last phase of this strategy, when using the audio to "home onto" the landmark, that either worked positively or negatively for participants. Whilst all landmarks were fixed in the environment, and GPS error affected only the determined location of the user, the result of any error could significantly alter the geographic relationship between the user and landmark. Although we used a highly accurate GPS unit, even a very small error in position (as is the case with any positioning technology) may put the determined user location on the opposite side of the landmark than the user really is. So instead of hearing the sound as coming from the right, where the landmark is, the user would hear it coming from the left. The effect of which is confusion of the user, who is relying on the information provided being accurate. This situation can still occur with the work on audio navigation previously described. However, it is the addition of physical landmarks that the user must determine he or she has found (a much more realistic task), rather than a user being told he or she has arrived when moving within an arbitrary radius around a location, that affects performance.

Fig. 3 shows this final stage for two different participants, each using the 30m condition from Study 1, attempting to home onto the same non-prominent landmark: a named bush. Fig. 3 (left) shows the trace for a user who had good accuracy and simply walked up to the landmark, and realised from the audio that he had passed it. He then turned and photographed it. Fig. 3 (right) however, shows the trace of a participant where the GPS determined location had placed her on the wrong side of the landmark. The participant spent a good deal of time searching the wrong side of the landmark because of this audio feedback. Eventually she realised from the map that the landmark must be behind her and moved her search. Afterwards she noted: "As I approached I waited for the sound and I tried to follow it. Sometimes it was helpful, but other times it was really confusing. That is why I made the mistakes. I was looking at the map and it was showing one way, but the audio was showing another way". Of all of the successfully identified non-prominent landmarks, 25% showed evidence of users searching in the wrong location due to audio feedback. However, we believe instances of audio mis-direction to be greater than this, as some participants quickly realised that the audio was indicating the incorrect direction and ignored it: "Sometimes it was telling you to turn left or right when it was clearly not the right way. So you would hear it in the left when it looked like it was to the right. It was more problematic when you got really close".

Therefore whilst audio could be useful, it could also be misleading. In such cases re-designing the audio to provide less direction fidelity to the user is likely to avoid misdirected searches, such as in Fig. 3 (right). Audio should inform users they are in the correct area, but that no more assistance can be provided.

6   Design Implications

From both the quantitative and qualitative results, we have contributed to knowledge of auditory navigation in three areas:

Maps and Audio: Users did not rely solely on either map or audio to reach the landmarks. Rather, they described how the map was used at the start of each trial, with the audio taking over to help home onto the landmark. When used with a map, audio navigation is only likely to be employed when in the immediate vicinity of the target. The always on audio condition, similar to existing work (e.g. [1]), was found to be unhelpful when a map was also provided.

Prominent Landmarks: Where a landmark is prominent in the environment audio is unlikely to be useful to home onto it. Users often did not hear any audio when searching for prominent landmarks. Although audio may be useful to confirm any doubt the landmark is correct. However, it should be noted that the aspect by which a user approaches a landmark may also affect its prominence. A building that is prominent when approached from the front, may be non-prominent when approached from the rear [14].

Audio Feedback: When correlating a virtual auditory landmark with a real, physical landmark, especially if that landmark is small, even minor gps error can have a large impact on performance. In many cases we saw the user search in the wrong direction (either searching to the left when the landmark was to the right, or vice-versa) because the audio indicated, due to positioning inaccuracy, that as the correct direction. Previous studies (see Section 2), which have used virtual landmarks without a physical manifestation, have not shown this to be an issue. However, where the user is searching for physical landmarks the audio should degrade gracefully when the determined user location to the landmark approaches that of the GPS error. This will avoid providing misleading information. How to best design audio to do this remains an open question.

7 Conclusions

Through two studies we have contributed to understanding the advantages and issues of spatialised audio for pedestrian navigation. We have shown how searching for physical landmarks, rather than only virtual auditory landmarks, affects performance, and how audio navigation can be integrated with other aids - such as maps. Whilst, as with prior work, auditory navigation was subjectively useful, it conferred no significant quantative improvement over a map. Whilst there may be additional reasons why this is the case, we have identified that presenting only directional auditory feedback can cause significant issues in performance when searching for real, physical landmarks. Such issues have not been previously uncovered by the literature, and we hope to motivate future work on spatialised auditory navigation to allow a full understanding of its use. In turn this will allow future researchers to provide rich and diverse auditory navigation experiences.

Acknowledgements. This work was supported by EU FP7 No.224675 "Haptimap". We thank Charlotte Magnusson, Kirre Rassmus-Gröhn and Delphine Szymczak for their helpful suggestions in the development of this work.

References

1. Strachan, S., Eslambolchilar, P., Murray-Smith, R., Hughes, S., O'Modhrain, S.: GpsTunes: controlling navigation via audio feedback. In: Proceedings of MobileHCI 2005, pp. 275–278. ACM, New York (2005)
2. Allen, G.L.: Spatial Abilities, Cognitive Maps, and Wayfinding: Bases for Individual Differences in Spatial Cognition and Behavior. In: Wayfinding Behaviour, pp. 46–80 (1999)
3. Pielot, M., Poppinga, B., Heuten, W., Boll, S.: 6th senses for everyone!: the value of multimodal feedback in handheld navigation aids. In: Proceedings of ICMI 2011, pp. 65–72. ACM, New York (2011)
4. Holland, S., Morse, D.R., Gedenryd, H.: AudioGPS: Spatial Audio Navigation with a Minimal Attention Interface. Personal Ubiquitous Computing 6(4), 253–259 (2002)
5. Jones, M., Jones, S., Bradley, G., Warren, N., Bainbridge, D., Holmes, G.: ON-TRACK: Dynamically adapting music playback to support navigation. Personal Ubiquitous Computing 12(7), 513–525 (2008)
6. Stahl, C.: The roaring navigator: a group guide for the zoo with shared auditory landmark display. In: Proceedings of MobileHCI 2007, pp. 383–386. ACM, New York (2007)
7. Walker, B.N., Lindsay, J.: Navigation Performance With a Virtual Auditory Display: Effects of Beacon Sound, Capture Radius, and Practice. Human Factors. The Journal of the Human Factors and Ergonomics Society 48(2), 265–278
8. McGookin, D., Brewster, S., Priego, P.: Audio Bubbles: Employing Non-speech Audio to Support Tourist Wayfinding. In: Altinsoy, M.E., Jekosch, U., Brewster, S. (eds.) HAID 2009. LNCS, vol. 5763, pp. 41–50. Springer, Heidelberg (2009)
9. Vazquez-Alvarez, Y., Oakley, I., Brewster, S.: Auditory display design for exploration in mobile audio-augmented reality. Personal and Ubiquitous Computing, 1–13 (2011)
10. Brown, B., Chalmers, M.: Tourism and Mobile Technology. In: 8th European Conference on CSCW, Helsinki, Finland, pp. 335–354. Kluwer Academic (2003)
11. Michon, P.-E., Denis, M.: When and Why Are Visual Landmarks Used in Giving Directions? In: Montello, D.R. (ed.) COSIT 2001. LNCS, vol. 2205, pp. 292–305. Springer, Heidelberg (2001)
12. Seager, W., Fraser, D.S.: Comparing physical, automatic and manual map rotation for pedestrian navigation. In: Proceedings of CHI 2007, pp. 767–776. ACM, New York (2007)
13. Kozhevnikov, M., Hegarty, M.: A dissociation between object manipulation spatial ability and spatial orientation ability. Memory & Cognition 29(5), 745–756 (2001)
14. Caduff, D., Timpf, S.: On the assessment of landmark salience for human navigation. Cognitive Processing 9(4), 249–267 (2008)
15. Crossan, A., Murray-Smith, R., Brewster, S., Kelly, J., Musizza, B.: Gait phase effects in mobile interaction. In: Extended Proceedings of CHI 2005, pp. 1312–1315. ACM, New York (2005)
16. Ritchie, J., Spencer, L.: Qualitative Data Analysis for Applied Policy Research. In: Bryman, A., Burgess, R. (eds.) Analysing Qualitative Data, pp. 173–194. Routledge, London (1993)

Supporting Sounds: Design and Evaluation
of an Audio-Haptic Interface

Emma Murphy[1,*], Camille Moussette[2], Charles Verron[3,**],
and Catherine Guastavino[1]

[1] Centre for Interdisciplinary Research in Music Media & Technology and School
of Information Studies, McGill University, Canada
emma.murphy@dcu.ie
[2] Umeå Institute of Design, Sweden
[3] Laboratoire de Mécanique et d'Acoustique de Marseille, France

Abstract. The design and evaluation of a multimodal interface is presented in order to investigate how spatial audio and haptic feedback can be used to convey the navigational structure of a virtual environment. The non-visual 3D virtual environment is composed of a number of parallel planes with either horizontal or vertical orientations. The interface was evaluated using a target-finding task to explore how auditory feedback can be used in isolation or combined with haptic feedback for navigation. Twenty-three users were asked to locate targets using auditory feedback in the virtual structure across both horizontal and vertical orientations of the planes, with and without haptic feedback. Findings from the evaluation experiment reveal that users performed the task faster in the bi-modal conditions (with combined auditory and haptic feedback) with a horizontal orientation of the virtual planes.

Keywords: Auditory feedback, Haptic feedback, Target-finding, User Evaluation.

1 Introduction

Despite ongoing research on the evaluation of systems that employ audio-haptic feedback, there is still much to be explored in the context of human-computer interaction. The present study investigates the relative contribution of audio and audio-haptic cues on performance and perceived usability, using a non-visual target finding task. Previous research has investigated the addition of haptics to visual interfaces for target-finding [1, 2]. Kim and Kwon [3] implemented a haptic and audio grid in order to enhance recognition for ambiguous visual depth cues. The authors implemented a haptic vertical grid and pitch variation to convey a target location to users and subsequent evaluations revealed that the multimodal cues increased precision, particularly in the vertical axis [3]. Magnusson and Grohn [4] evaluated a set of audio-haptic

---

* Currently at Dublin City University, Ireland.
** Currently at REVES-INRIA, Sophia Antipolis, France.

C. Magnusson, D. Szymczak, and S. Brewster (Eds.): HAID 2012, LNCS 7468, pp. 11–20, 2012.
© Springer-Verlag Berlin Heidelberg 2012

feedback cues using a Phantom Omni haptic device with 3D auditory cues for visually impaired to locate non-visual objects in a virtual environment using a memory game task. Findings from this study show that this technique of 3D sound mapping aided users' understating of the spatial layout of the virtual space. Furthermore the addition of 3D sound cues to a virtual interface with visual and haptic cues was shown to improve collaboration between users [4] by enhancing awareness of ongoing work between participants. In [5] an audio-haptic interface was evaluated to investigate if users could integrate information from audio and haptic sensory channels in order to achieve a target selection task. The results of this study revealed that users had a preference for haptic feedback, even when audio could be considered better suited to the task. Ménélas et al. [7] investigated the addition of audio, haptic and combined audio-haptic to enhance target finding tasks in visual 3D environments with multiple and obscured targets. The findings from this study illustrated that haptic feedback and combined audio haptic feedback were more effective when compared to the audio-only condition to enhance the visual cues. The use of a full loudspeaker array is not always feasible for the design of user interfaces and binaural synthesis of 3D sound [8] over headphones is often more appropriate. Gonot [9] et al. has investigated the use of binaural synthesis in comparison to stereophonic implementations for navigating in constrained virtual environments. Findings from this study reveal that binaural synthesis can yield better results in terms of usability, cognitive load and subjective evaluation. Wall et al. [10] explored the potential of haptic feedback in the form of virtual magnetic cues to enhance a visual target finding task in comparison to the addition of stereo visual graphics. The magnetic effect applied to draw the user towards the target did not enhance participant's temporal performance although it did improve accuracy, while the stereo graphic condition improved both user accuracy and timings. Hwang et al [11] have illustrated that haptic force feedback in the form of gravity wells can enhance user performance for both time and error rates in multi target-finding tasks.

2   Methods

The virtual environment was composed of five equally spaced parallel planes. Practical applications for this virtual structure include the design of a non-visual menu or browser interface. By including five planes, the structure represented an interesting stack-like configuration, and it matched reasonably well with the physical constraints of the haptic device. Furthermore a restricted visual space could be increased on a small screen device by using the virtual planes to represent alternative views. Two configurations have been considered, with either horizontal or vertical planes. A virtual target was located at a random location on one of the planes as shown in Figure 1.

Fig. 1. Structure of 3D planes in both vertical and horizontal orientations with target located randomly on one of the planes

In order to find the target the user had to navigate through the planes and identify which one contained the target. A virtual bowed sound was played when the target and the stylus of the haptic device were located on the same plane (horizontal or vertical, according to the configuration). By identifying the position of the virtual sound source, the listener could navigate on the plane and locate the target. The aim of the experiment was to compare the differences in usability and navigation using the two different orientations of the virtual structure: horizontal and vertical, and the two different types of feedback: audio and audio-haptic. Specifically, we investigated whether it would be possible to navigate the interface and find the target without the support of the haptic planes. Due to the fact that the interface was not designed with redundant information between modalities we hypothesized that it would be more difficult for users to navigate the environment without haptic feedback.

2.1   Haptic Feedback

Haptic effects were designed and controlled using H3D[1], an open source haptic graphic API based on X3D[2], and a Phantom Omni haptic device from Sensable Technologies Inc. This desktop unit offers 6 degrees of freedom with a stylus-type grip and provides a workspace area of 160 W x 120 H x 70 D mm.

The five virtual planes were positioned at 10 mm intervals centered on the device's workspace origin. The planes were large enough to completely fill the workspace area on the other axes. This compact arrangement allows us to rotate the stack while keeping the spacing and haptic configuration intact. The interval distance of 10 mm between the planes seemed appropriate and adequate after initial pilot testing. It was the largest value possible to work with both orientations (the Omni depth axis offers only 70 mm of travel). Beyond our rendered haptic features, the users were naturally limited to the mechanical limits of the device in all three axes. The haptic feedback was active only on the planes and the target. Between the planes no forces were applied. The haptic rendering used a magnetic effect from Sensable's OpenHaptics library (MagneticSurface[3]) to create semi-rigid surfaces to hold users to the five planes while

---

[1]   http://www.h3d.org

[2]   http://www.web3d.org/x3d/specifications

[3]   http://www.h3dapi.org/modules/apidoc/html/
      classH3D_1_1MagneticSurface.html

they were navigating the virtual environment. The magnetic effect consisted of forces (F=-kx) generated in order to keep the point of device's stylus on the defined surfaces. When the pointer was pulled outside a specific delta distance from the planes, it was freed from the magnetic attraction. In our experiment, the haptic planes were built with a stiffness index of 0.4 and 2 mm for the snap distance setting. The randomly positioned target consisted of a 4 mm radius sphere with a high surface friction value and no magnetic force applied. Contact between the pointer and the target's surface automatically registered the successful completion of the task and triggered the corresponding auditory cue. Note that the Phantom Omni can produce a maximum exertable force of 3.3 Newtons. Only the positional X, Y and Z data of the arm were used for the study. The device was situated on a desk and we left the grip position of the stylus open to the participants.

2.2   Audio Feedback

The auditory interface was created using a set of sound samples, triggered according to the actions of the user. We based the choice of audio samples on a musical metaphor with a string instrument. More specifically, the haptic movement through the planes was complemented by a plucked sound, and movements on a given plane were sonified by a smooth bowing sound. Cello samples (retrieved from www.freesound.org/) were chosen over other string instrument samples as the lower register was considered less obtrusive to the listener. Each plane was assigned a plucked pitch corresponding to the first 5 notes of a major scale mapped to the ascending plane number (A3, B3, C#3, D3, E3). Five plucked sounds (corresponding to the five notes) were used to inform the user of a plane crossing. A continuous bowed cello sound was played while the user was on the correct plane (i.e., the plane with the target) until they located the target. The pitch of the bowed sound was the same as the plucked sound for that plane level. Finally, when the user successfully located the target, a distinctive bowed chord auditory cue was played[4].

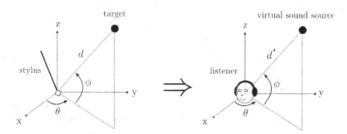

Fig. 2. The "ears in hand" metaphor: a virtual sound source is spatialized to simulate the target position relative to the haptic device stylus. The direction and distance (with a scaling factor) are reproduced with binaural synthesis.

---

[4] A video demo (with monophonic sound rendering) is available at
http://www.computing.dcu.ie/~emurphy/video/Audio-Haptic.mov

The bowed sound was spatialized using binaural synthesis to guide the user on the plane and find the target. We used the "ears in hand" metaphor similar to that reported in [4]. The target was simulated as a virtual sound source, while the stylus (corresponding to listener's hand) represented the center of listener's head. More specifically, the azimuth θ, elevation φ and the distance d of the target were calculated in a coordinate system (x,y,z) whose origin was attached to the point of the haptic device's stylus (see Figures 1 and 2). Then the bowed cello sound was spatialized with coordinates (θ, φ, d') in a listener-centric system (Figure 2). The relatively small size of the Phantom Omni workspace (160 W x 120 H x 70 D mm) was compensated by a scaling factor of 60 for simulating the virtual source distance relative to the listener, i.e., d'=60d. The target-stylus distance being comprised between approximately 0 and 0.2 m, the corresponding source-listener distance varied between 0 and 12 m. Note that the orientation of the axes (x,y,z) always matched the orientation of the five planes in the virtual environment, and did not depend on the orientation of the stylus itself.

The Spatialisateur (v3.4.1.1) developed by IRCAM for Max/MSP was used for binaural sound rendering over headphones [12]. Directional cues θ and φ were simulated with Head Related Transfer Function (HRTF) filtering based on KEMAR measurements. The distance cue d' was simulated by attenuating the direct sound with a gain: $g = 1/d'$ if d' >1 m otherwise g=1. The cello sound source level was calibrated to approximately 50 dB-SPL for the reference distance of 1m. For a source-listener distance d' inferior to 1 m (i.e., a stylus-target distance d inferior to 1.6 cm) the virtual source was moved on the upper hemisphere, reaching φ=+90 degrees when d'=0 m. Artificial reverberation was used to improve the distance perception and enhance the externalisation of the virtual source [13]. We choose a 2 second reverberation time and a global reverberation gain of -24dB. Since the source-listener distance varied from 0 to 12 m in the experiment, this settings lead to direct/reverberant signal ratios ranging from 24 to 10 dB. Doppler and air absorption effects were not simulated in this study. As the sound played only when the target and the stylus were located on the same plane, in the horizontal configuration the elevation of the virtual source was always 0 degree and the azimuth varied continuously between -180 to +180 degrees; in the vertical configuration, the azimuth of the virtual source was either -90 or +90 degrees, and the elevation varied continuously between -90 and +90 degrees.

2.3   Experimental Design

The experimental design was based on the following independent variables;

- Feedback: audio only, audio-haptic
- Orientation of the virtual planes: vertical, horizontal

This resulted in four experimental conditions: Audio-Haptic Vertical, Audio-Haptic Horizontal, Audio-Only Vertical, Audio-Only Horizontal.

2.3.1   Participants and Procedure
Twenty-three participants volunteered for the study, 20 males and 3 females between the ages of 24 and 55 (mean age: 32, SD: 8.2). Participants were either involved in an eNTERFACE '08 workshop or part of the wider research community at LIMSI,

CNRS, France, involved in audio, computer science or engineering related research. While most users had experience testing and working with non-speech sound only 6 users reported prior experience testing or working with a haptic device.

Participants were provided with both a short training introduction and a practical trial session before beginning the main experiment. The initial training introduction involved presenting a visual description of the virtual structure (as represented in Figure 1). While the entire experiment was non-visual it was considered useful to show the users a visual representation of the virtual structure so that they could visualise the task mentally. However, users were not given any information about the 3D audio mappings or the haptic feedback.

In a practical training session, users were presented with 8 trials, 2 of each condition. Users were asked to navigate the planes, find the plane with the target and locate that target. For the main experiment participants were presented with 44 trials (11 per condition), except for the first 3 participants who completed 40 trials (10 per condition). The order of presentation of both orientation and feedback were radomised across trials. The target position within and across planes was also randomised. In order to move onto the next trial participants were asked to press a button on the Phantom Omni stylus when they were ready to move on. Timings were recorded from this point until the user located the target. There was an automatic detection of the end of task target location. User trajectories across and within the virtual planes were also recorded. Participants were also asked to complete a post-task questionnaire concerning perceived effectiveness and ease of use of the audio-haptic cues and the participant's cognitive strategies for finding the target.

3   Results

Users successfully located the target across all trials for the audio-haptic condition. In the audio-only condition, 4 users failed to locate the target for a combined total of 10 trials (6 horizontal, 4 vertical). Their timings were recorded for the unsuccessful trials (Average: 167s) but not included in the data for completion times. Furthermore, 62 trials out of 1000 trials were excluded from the data analysis due to technical difficulties.

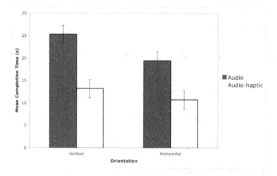

Fig. 3. Mean completion times for vertical and horizontal orientations across both audio only and audio-haptic conditions. Error bars display Standard Error.

Figure 3 illustrates the mean completion times for each condition. A repeated measures factorial ANOVA for completion times revealed significant effects of orientation and feedback. The time taken for users to complete the task in the horizontal condition was significantly less than that of vertical condition ($F(1, 936) = 6.1$, $p=0.02$). In addition, completion times for the audio-only condition were significantly longer than those of the audio-haptic condition ($F(1, 936) = 49.3$, $p<0.001$). Furthermore, post-hoc tests revealed a significant difference between the vertical and horizontal orientations for both audio-only ($t(243) = -2.94$, p two-tailed $=0.004$) and audio-haptic conditions ($t(228) = -3.07$, p two-tailed $=0.002$). There were no interaction effects between feedback and orientation.

3.1 Trajectory Analysis

We recorded the angular change of the arm of the Phantom Omni for each trial and each participant to gather information on the user's navigation path in addition to their completion times. A repeated measures factorial ANOVA for angular change revealed a significant main effect of orientation ($F(1,936) = 5.6$, $p<0.05$) and main effect of feedback ($F(1,936)=18.0$, $p<0.0001$)). There were no interaction effects between feedback and orientation. The mean angular data confirms the time data analysis in that the user trajectory paths were longer in the vertical orientation for both feedback conditions.

We also recorded the number of times that the users crossed planes when searching for the plane with the target for each trial. A repeated measures factorial ANOVA for mean plane crossings revealed a significant main effect of feedback ($F(1,936) = 39.0$, $p<0.0001$) but no main effect of orientation. No interaction effects were observed between feedback and orientation conditions. It is interesting that orientation did not have a significant effect on the mean plane crossings before users identified the target. The mean number of plane crossings are almost the same for both vertical (5.6) and horizontal orientations (5.7) in the audio-haptic feedback condition. Considering that there were 5 planes in the design, these ratings illustrate that the magnetic haptic effect was effective to control the participant's movements in both conditions. The greater mean number of crossings in the audio only conditions (14.7) demonstrated that this it was more difficult to remain on a given plane without haptic feedback, especially in the vertical condition.

3.2 Post-task Feedback, Observations, User Comments

In post-task questionnaires users were asked to rate the audio, haptic and combination of audio haptic cues on a scale of 1-5 (5 as the highest value) in terms of effectiveness and ease of use. A one-way ANOVA revealed a significant effect for ease of use ratings on the three types of feedback ($F(2, 67= 8.7$, $p<.001$). Post-hoc tests revealed a significant difference between ratings for effectiveness for haptic and audio-haptic cue conditions ($t(44) = 2,3$, p two-tailed $=0.03$), with audio-haptic cues perceived as significantly more effective than haptic cues. A one-way ANOVA revealed no significant effect for ease of use ratings across the three types of feedback.

It should be noted that participants never experienced the haptic feedback in isolation. As a result, some users interpreted rating the haptic cue as evaluating the haptic feedback in terms of whether the task would have been possible with haptic feedback alone. Overall the subjective feedback for effectiveness and ease of use of cues were relatively high (Mean Rating: 3.8, SD: 0.4) and in verbal feedback as part of the post-task questionnaires, users reported a pleasurable experience interacting with the virtual environment and found the task enjoyable.

As part of post-task questionnaires users were asked to describe their strategies for finding the target using the multimodal interface. Most users described a process of first navigating the virtual space to determine the orientation of the planes, then using the auditory cues to first determine the correct plane and concentrate on the location cue to find the target. From observation the most efficient users were those who immediately grasped the structure of the virtual environment and understood the 3D audio cues. In the post-task questionnaires 13 out of 23 users included descriptions of the spatial audio cues as part of their strategy for locating the target. From questionnaire analysis the remainder of the users did not refer to the fact that the cues were spatialized and instead commented on the changes in intensity for the location cues. In terms of the 3D audio rendering, no front-back or up-down reversals were mentioned by participants in the post-test questionnaire, nor did we observe any inversions in the analysis of the trajectories. Such reversals are typical artifacts of static binaural synthesis that can be reduced by head-tracking [13]. Head movements were not tracked in our experiment, but the "ears in hand" metaphor allowed subjects to explore dynamically the auditory space by means of the haptic stylus. It is possible that this exploration helped reducing the front-back and up-down confusions by providing dynamic localization cues to the listener.

4   Discussion

Our findings provide support for our research hypothesis, that haptic feedback improves performance of a target-finding task. The highly significant difference in completion times between audio vs. audio haptic feedback can be accounted for by the design of the interface, as the haptic cues were designed to support the auditory interface without any redundant information. Although users found it more difficult to remain on the virtual planes, it should be noted that they were able to complete the task using the auditory cues within a reasonable length of time without haptic feedback. But users may have been applying the mental model of the virtual structure previously constructed during the training session or previous trials using audio-haptic condition. This would need to be further investigated in a separate audio-only evaluation study.

The significant difference of completion times in the horizontal for both audio and audio-haptic conditions is a reflection of the mappings for the binaural rendering of 3D sound as this was the main cue to allow users locate the target. An explanation for the longer completion times in the vertical orientation is that users were relying on elevation cues   (with non-individualized HRTF) to navigate the surface of the planes in this condition. This finding is in agreement with previous studies that have illustrated that participants find elevation cues difficult to perceive [14]. From this finding it is possible to recommend that in the design of auditory interfaces using 3D sound to convey a virtual 3D space, it is better to map 3D binaural rendering along a horizontal plane. Vertical movements may better be conveyed through other non-speech auditory parameters such as pitch or intensity. Some users alternated their hand position to compensate for the changing orientation of the planes. It should be acknowledged that there are physiological constraints in terms of the gestural control of the haptic device and this could have an effect on user performance in the vertical orientation.

5   Conclusions and Future Work

We foresee that the design idea of virtual planes developed during this experiment could be favorably adapted to ungrounded interfaces like portable devices where small screen sizes are often a limiting factor in building complex interfaces. The haptic cues are generated from the device itself as it moves and changes orientation. The use of an expanded navigation space using the proposed 3D plane structure with audio and haptic feedback provides interesting capabilities for developing meaningful interfaces that are contextually relevant and engaging. Simple but very valuable haptic feedback could support browsing of various layers of data (maps, menu structures, subsets of a larger collection, etc) or enhance selection task from a few discrete items with haptic detents through 3D space, like a scroll wheel on a computer mouse. Haptic layers could be enhanced by using spatial audio to render options not accessible in a limited visual display. For example the 3D spatial audio design presented in this paper could be extended to include audio pan-and-zoom techniques proposed in [15]. The target finding interface could be exploited to test a combination of audio, haptic and visual cues to implement a collaborative game for blind and sighted users. Interaction design using audio and haptic feedback has the potential to create learning objects to include children otherwise marginalised as a result of disabilities such as visual impairment or learning disabilities.

Acknowledgments. This study was supported by an NSERC-SRO team grant on ENACTIVE Interfaces (P.I.: M. Wanderley), We would like to thank Orange Labs, Dr. Antoine Gonot and Dr. Ilja Frissen.

References

1. Oakley, I., McGee, M.R., Brewster, S., Gray, P.: Putting the feel in look and feel. In: Proceedings of the SIGCHI Conference on Human Factors in Computing Systems (CHI 2000), pp. 415–422 (2000)
2. Wall, S.A., Paynter, K., Shillito, A.M., Wright, M., Scali, S.: The effect of haptic feedback and stereo graphics in a 3d target acquisition. In: Proceedings of Eurohaptics, Edinburgh, UK, July 8-10 (2002)

3. Kim, S.-C., Kwon, D.-S.: Haptic and Sound Grid for Enhanced Positioning in a 3-D Virtual Environment. In: Oakley, I., Brewster, S. (eds.) HAID 2007. LNCS, vol. 4813, pp. 98–109. Springer, Heidelberg (2007)

4. Magnusson, C., Danielsson, H., Rassmus-Gröhn, K.: Non Visual Haptic Audio Tools for Virtual Environments. In: McGookin, D., Brewster, S. (eds.) HAID 2006. LNCS, vol. 4129, pp. 111–120. Springer, Heidelberg (2006)

5. Moll, J., Huang, Y., Sallnas, E.: Audio makes a difference in haptic collaborative virtual environments. Interact. Comput. 22(6), 544–555 (2010)

6. Picinali, L., Menelas, B., Katz, B., Bourdot, P.: Evaluation of a Haptic/Audio System for 3-D Targeting Tasks. In: Proceedings of the 128th Convention of the Audio Engineering Society, London, UK (2010)

7. Ménélas, B., Picinali, L., Katz, B., Bourdot, P.: Audio haptic feedbacks in a task of targets acquisition. In: IEEE Symposium on 3D User Interfaces (3DUI 2010), Waltham, USA, pp. 51–54 (2010)

8. Blauert, J.: Spatial hearing: the psychophysics of human sound localization. MIT Press, Cambridge (1997)

9. Gonot, A., Chateau, N., Emerit, M.: Usability of 3-D Sound for Navigation in a Constrained Virtual Environment. In: Proceedings of the Audio Engineering Society (AES) Convention (2006)

10. Wall, S.A., Paynter, K., Shillito, A.M., Wright, S., Scali, M.: The effect of haptic feedback and stereo graphics in a 3d target acquisition. In: Proceedings of Eurohaptics, Edinburgh, UK, pp. 23–29 (2002)

11. Hwang, F., Keates, S., Langdon, P., Clarkson, J.: Multiple haptic targets for motion-impaired computer users. In: Proceedings of CHI 2003, Florida, USA, pp. 41–48 (2003)

12. Jot, J.-M.: Real-time Spatial processing of sounds for music, multimedia and interactive human-computer interfaces. ACM Multimedia Systems Journal 7(1), 55–69 (1999)

13. Begault, D.R., Wenzel, E.M., Anderson, M.R.: Direct Comparison of the Impact of Head Tracking, Reverberation, and Individualized Head-Related Transfer Functions on the Spatial Perception of a Virtual Speech Source. Journal of the Audio Engineering Society 49(10) (2001)

14. Lokki, T., Grohn, M.: Navigation with auditory cues in a virtual environment. IEEE Multimedia 12(2) (2005)

15. Bouchara, T., Katz, B., Jacquemin, C., Guastavino, C.: Audio-visual renderings for multimedia navigation. In: Proceedings of the 16th International Conference on Auditory Display, Washington, DC (2010)

A Haptic-Audio Interface for Acquiring Spatial Knowledge about Apartments

Junlei Yu and Christopher Habel

Department of Informatics, University of Hamburg, Germany
{jyu,habel}@informatik.uni-hamburg.de

Abstract. In selecting an apartment for residence, floor plans are a common source of relevant information. For visually impaired people, adequate floor plans are widely missing. This paper introduces a haptic-audio assistance system, which is designed and implemented to help visually impaired people to acquire the layout of novel small-scale apartments. Virtual 2.5-D floor plan models are made according to—traditional visual—floor plans. Haptic force feedback will be rendered when users explore the virtual model by a PHANToM Omni device. During the exploration, auditory assistance information about floor plans, either by speech or by sonification, is invoked by entering into prescribed areas, which are placed on the inner contour of rooms. Two user studies are presented which demonstrate the usability of the haptic-audio interface. In particular, reinforcement and extra positive influence brought by the employment of multiple modes in audio perception channel is confirmed.

Keywords: Spatial Knowledge Acquisition, Virtual Haptics, Haptic-Audio Floor plan, Sonification.

1 Introduction

The use of spatial knowledge is ubiquitous in our daily life. For example, the task of selecting a residence to rent is not possible to be accomplished without spatial knowledge of the apartment. Floor plans, which inform people about the apartment's overall layout as well as of the individual rooms and the relationships between them, are commonly used external representations of indoor environments. For visually impaired people, the information presented by traditional floor plans is not directly accessible. In order to overcome these limits, appropriate substitution is required.

Tactile maps are effective means for blind and visually impaired people to acquire knowledge of their urban environment. As Espinosa and colleagues [2] point out, tactile maps can potentially increase the autonomy of blind and visually impaired people. Whereas visual perception supports comprehension processes, which switch between global and local aspects of a graphical representation, haptic perception has a more local and in particular a more sequential character. Thus, compared to visual maps, one drawback of tactile maps is the restriction of the haptic sense regarding the possibility of simultaneous perception of information (for an overview see [8]). In the

C. Magnusson, D. Szymczak, and S. Brewster (Eds.): HAID 2012, LNCS 7468, pp. 21–30, 2012.
© Springer-Verlag Berlin Heidelberg 2012

case of haptic map-reading, the sequential character of haptic exploration demands additional effort in integrating of information over time. As a consequence, this leads to limitations in building up cognitive maps, such as more sparse density of information and less sufficient survey knowledge.

The increasing availability of haptic interfaces for human-computer interaction (HCI) offers a large variety of prospects for training and assisting blind people. In particular, by the means of such devices (for example, the PHANToM® Omni) it is possible to realize map-like representations of physical environments that are HCI-counterparts to traditional tactile maps. To overcome the 'integrating spatial information over time' problems of haptic exploration, providing additional information, such as auditory assistance through the auditory channel, has been proven to be helpful [7]. Several multimodal systems have been developed that use sounds or prerecorded speech when objects on tactile maps are touched (e.g., [9], [18], [20]) or that generate sentences aware of the current act of exploration [6], [7]).

In contrast to maps, floor plans, which are a kindred type of graphical representations, play up to now a minor role in the development of haptic—or even audio-haptic—interfaces (but, see e.g., [15], [13], [5]). Whereas most maps of urban environments have 'paths' as primary graphical entities and thus line-following constitutes the main haptic exploration strategy [3], floor plans possess regions, depicting rooms or hallways, as primary graphical entities and border-following as main haptic exploration strategy. This contrast between maps and floor plans, which is based on the graphical inventory and the consequential exploration procedures, restricts the portability from haptic-audio maps to haptic-audio floor plans.

In this paper, we introduce a haptic-audio interface addressing floor plan based spatial-knowledge acquisition of apartments to be usable by blind and visually impaired people (see Fig. 1). The remainder of the paper is organized as follows: In Section 2 we describe the main objectives of the proposed system and the 'division of labor' among the haptic and the auditory (sub-)modalities. In Section 3 we present results of two experiments—performed with blindfolded participants—concerning the shape comprehension and the processing of information about windows. We decided to test the system with blindfolded sighted participants rather than with blind or visually impaired participants because of two reasons. Firstly, blind and visually impaired people are not always familiar with floor plans. Thus effects of becoming accustomed to floor plans can be excluded with blindfolded sighted participants. Secondly, one goal of the studies reported here was to develop, refine and evaluate different principles of multimodal floor-plan exploration before testing the system with visually impaired people (cf. [7] regarding map-exploration assistance). Follow-up experiments with blind and visually impaired people are planed.

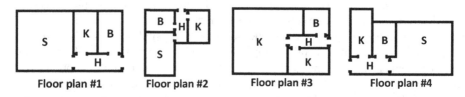

Fig. 1. Virtual floor plans employed in Experiment 1

2   Towards Haptic-Audio Modeling of Simple Floor Plans

Using floor plans to get an initial impression of an apartment provide various spatial properties of the rooms and their spatial configuration, such as size and shape of rooms, the position of doors or the location of windows. To sum up, a tactile floor plan should—similar to tactile maps—provide a blind or visually impaired person with the possibility to build up a mental representation of the apartment in question by haptic exploration of a virtual model. Beyond acquiring knowledge about the individual rooms, a 'picture' of the apartment as a whole should also be possible to be constructed. Last but not least, for living in an apartment, functional aspects of rooms are highly important, e.g. 'being a bathroom / the hallway', 'having a window', etc.). Appropriate information can be provided by the haptic-audio interface.

Various studies on tactile-map use and similar applications—see, for example, [9], [12], [15]—give evidence, that maps and floor plans for blind readers should be limited in detail and complexity. To constrain the variations of our empirical studies, we chose the following constraints on floor plans and thus on the depicted apartments to be explored by blindfolded people. For the experiment 1 (see Section 3.1) the constraints are as follows (see Fig. 1): (1) number of rooms: hallway and three function-rooms, bath, kitchen and sleeping room; (2) shape of rooms: rectangular vs. L-shapes; (3) size and proportion of rooms: sizes of rooms as well the proportion of side-lengths are limited to a small number of values; (4) accessibility: all function-rooms have a door to/from the hallway, there are no doors between function rooms (This—so-called—palm-structure avoids loops in exploring); (5) global shape:, i.e., shape of the apartment: rectangular vs. L-shapes.

2.1   Haptic (re-)presentations

In accordance to other approaches for (re-)presenting maps, floor plans or room plans to be explored haptically ([5], [9], [15]), we use virtual 2.5-D plans—realized with the open source library Chai3D—explored via a Sensable PHANToM Omni force feedback device. In our virtual haptic floor plans, only two elementary entities are represented by force feedback. Solid borders are used for 'walls' of the apartment, and two end-to-end emerged ovals stand for 'doors' (see the training floor plan in Fig. 2).

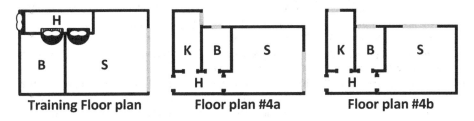

Fig. 2. Virtual floor plans (with windows: gray shaded) used in Experiment 2

When the haptic interaction point touches different components of the virtual floor plan, either stable linear force feedback or wavy force feedback is rendered accordingly. There are two types of 'walls', namely external walls, which define the global shape of the entire apartment, and internal walls, which form the boundaries of different functional areas, i.e. rooms. The external walls are 7 cm in height, and the internal walls are 2 cm, i.e. both types restrict leaving the room. Although there is no 'roof' on the top of the apartment constraining the exploration of the user, jumping over the walls to go from one area to another by lifting the stylus up has not be applied by the users. The two-oval design for the door enables the user to distinguish the door from 'open space' by perceiving wavy haptic stimuli from the stylus. The wavy stimuli are mild and smooth, so the users can detect the existence of the door, but they are still conscious of travelling in a linear track. The groove in the middle of the door helps the users to anchor themselves, and makes it easier to go through the doors.

2.2   From 'Haptic' to 'Haptic-Audio': The *Division of Labor* Advantage

As Sjöström et al. [15] in their pioneer prototype of virtual indoor environment describe, their users had high success in learning the correct number of rooms of an apartment, and even in an office-building scenario (with 18 rooms) a majority of their users were able to identify one specific room. This confirms that number-of-rooms problems are in the scope of haptic floor plan use. Additionally, explorations with respect to shape, size and proportion of rooms correspond to haptic capacities, are well investigated in haptic-perception research in general, namely perception of shape, length and orientation [16]. Researches on haptic-interfaces, and even specific investigations on tactile graphs, maps and floor plans for blind users correspond to these findings [12].

As mentioned above, knowledge about the function of individual rooms is essential for the user, and in addition, knowing the functional property of rooms decreases the effort and memory load for discrimination, i.e. for identifying, the rooms. In revisiting a room as well as for remembering the properties of a room after exploration, conceptual labels, as "bath room" have an advantage over complex spatial determiners as "the second room at the left side of the hallway" (Both specifications in quotes stand for internal representations of the user, not for natural language expressions.) To give the user this information, speech, i.e. the auditory modality, is more appropriate as the haptic modality (Braille).

A second field for haptic-audio multimodality we want to discuss in the following is the 'spatial overlap' of entities. Windows, which can be conceptualized as openings in walls, are visualized in standard floor plans mostly by shadowing, color-coding, etc. These conventions are not easy to transfer to tactile maps. In contrast to doors, whose tactile-map counterparts should be traversable in haptic explorations, windows should not be permeable. Due to the 'spatial-overlap view' on windows, namely that windows are parts of walls, haptic following of a wall is—for some parts of the wall—also the following of a window. Therefore, a separation of these exploration events is suitable: wall following is done haptically, window following is perceived by audition. In other words, the tasks are distributed to the haptic modality and the auditory modality based on principles of 'division of labor'. Furthermore, within the auditory modality, namely between speech and non-speech audio of different types

[11], also 'division of labor' principles should be in use. In our interface all the invoking areas for audio assistance cannot be felt by exploring the virtual haptic floor plan.

2.3   Audio Assistance: The Use of Speech and Sonification

Beyond standard visual-graphical interfaces, in particular auditory interfaces, using speech and sonification as two representational sub-modes for audio assistance, are successfully employed in multimodal human-computer interaction ([10], [11], [14]).

The floor plans used in Experiment 1 (see Section 3.1) use verbal labels, presented by speech, identifying rooms by their function. The audio assistance over room types is triggered by visiting an 'invoking area' (depicted by shaded half-circles and rectangles in Fig. 2: training floor plan). When the user goes back to the hallway from any other rooms, the system tells, "You are back in the hallway." Since all virtual apartments are rendered from realistic palm-structured residence apartment, the confirmation information of a second visit will only be given in the hallway.

The sonifications used in Experiment 2 (see Section 3.2) are designed to be continuous harmonic beeps, which start when the window areas are touched by the haptic interaction point. When there is only one window, the beep is pitched at 250 Hz.. In case of two windows in the same room, one will stay with 250 Hz, the other one will have 1000 Hz. So in the first place, the participants are supposed to be aware of the existence of the window(s) within possibly the shortest time and least mental effort. Then the users may integrate the speed of the their exploration with the duration of the beeps into an estimation of the length or proportion.

3   Experiments

Two user experiments are reported in this section. With Experiment 1, we tested a haptic-audio interface as a substitution of tactile floor plans. In Experiment 2, sonification for windows was employed as reinforcement of Experiment 1. Not only the results of the individual experiments but also the comparison of the results is reported.

3.1   Experiment 1

We conducted a repeated-measures experiment with four different virtual floor plans. Before the real experiment, all 20 participants (11 female, 9 male, mean age: 23.8 years, *SD*: 2.28 years, they were all university students having little or no experience with haptic force feedback devices) were trained how to operate the force-feedback device and how to deal with the experimental tasks. In the experiment, blindfolded participants had no time limit to explore each virtual floor plan till they claimed that they had learned the floor plan well enough. Then the participants were asked to produce a sketch of the floor plan in a 12 cm by 12 cm sized box printed on the answer sheet, and then to do a size-ordering task, which was to formulate a chain of inequations to present the relative size of all the four different rooms of the apartment. For example, "sleeping room > kitchen > bathroom = hallway" means: The sleeping room was the largest. The kitchen was the second largest. The bathroom had the same size as the hallway and they are the smallest.

Since variations in floor plan features have different influence on human recognition [4], in order to discard the order effect of the experimental conditions (four different virtual floor plans), the Latin Square Design (see [1]) was used.

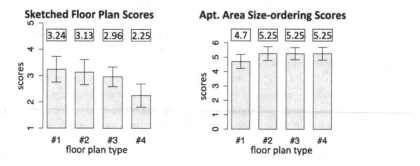

Fig. 3. Evaluation results of the sketch task and the size-ordering task (In this paper, all bar charts are modified with the mean values and the 95% confidence interval of them.)

The scores (range from 1 to 5) of the sketched floor plans are computed as a weighted sum considering five—separately scored—aspects: (NR) number of rooms, (LA) global layout/topology of the apartment, (GS) global shape of the apartment, (LS) local shape of the rooms and (PD) position of doors. The score function (aspects and weights) is based on an empirical study, in which 16 raters graded 64 sketched floor plans (see [19]). In this virtual floor plan experiment, the results show that the scoring of the sketches was significantly affected by the specific floor plan explored, $F(3,76) = 5.57$, $p < .05$, as the sketches of #1 are highest rated, then #2 and #3, and #4 the lowest. Post hoc tests using Bonferroni correction revealed that the performance of #1 was significantly better than that of #4, $p < .05$. This implies that L-shapedness had influence on sketching producing after the exploration virtual floor plan. The weakness revealed in the sketches of #3 and #4 was mainly resulted from taking the L-shaped sleeping rooms as rectangle.

To analyze the performance of the size-ordering task, the chain of inequations representing the size-ordering of the four rooms of the apartment was first decomposed into six binary inequations. The derived six binary inequations corresponding to the former chain of inequations example would be: "sleeping room > kitchen", "sleeping room > bathroom", "sleeping room > hallway", "kitchen > bathroom", "kitchen > hallway", and "bathroom = hallway". Answering each binary inequation correctly scored one point. So the total score of this task ranged from 0 to 6. The performance was fairly good and did not significantly change over the four different virtual floor plans, $F(3.76) = 1.51$, $p > .05$. The most common mistake was to regard a kitchen as bigger than the bathroom. Noticing the fact that in most residences the kitchen has larger area than the bathroom, we assume that participants' own experience has influence on the size-ordering task. The lower mean performance when floor plan #1 was explored could result from the fact that the kitchen, the bathroom and the hallway had very similar size, and further more the bathroom and the kitchen were equally sized, which lead to a comparably larger number of errors in the inequation chain.

With this experiment, we claim the possibility of acquiring relevant knowledge about small-scaled apartments, including the number of the rooms, the name of the rooms, the access of the rooms and the geometrical features of the rooms as well as that of the apartment as a whole

3.2   Experiment 2

Based on Experiment 1, the virtual floor plans of Experiment 2 were augmented by sonifying windows. For every original floor plan two different window configurations, named by "a" and "b", were implemented. There were two or three windows in each apartment, with at the most two windows in one room. The value of 'window-length to wall-length' ratio varied between 0.25 and 1 (seven ratios). The windows were always embedded in external walls of the apartment, as exemplified in Fig. 2. For experimental condition assignment, the virtual floor plans in a specific Latin Square were either all with window configuration "a", or with window configuration "b" (Table 1). The total number of virtual floor plans with each window configuration was counterbalanced. After each exploration, the participants went through the same tasks as in Experiment1, and in addition, they gave their opinion on the importance of information about windows in a questionnaire at end of the experiment.

Table 1. Experimental Condition assignment of the Experiment 2

Subjects	Experimental Configurations			
Sub 1	#1a	#4a	#2a	#3a
Sub 2	#2a	#1a	#3a	#4a
Sub 3	#3a	#2a	#4a	#1a
Sub 4	#4a	#3a	#1a	#2a

According to the outcomes so far, all 8 participants (3 female, 5 male, mean age: 23.4 years, *SD*: 2.7 years, they were all university students having little or no experience with haptic force feedback devices, and had not participated in Experiment 1) succeeded in telling the correct number of windows in any room, as well as the total number of windows in the apartment, and they located the windows to the walls correctly. When the value of the window-wall proportion in the virtual floor plan increases, the reproduced proportion in the sketches climbs up. The windows to wall proportion is not very precisely reproduced. In answering the questionnaire, participants usually claimed that the existence and the number of the windows were important to them whereas the exact position and the size of the windows were not. In spite of the report, the sketched window-wall ratio was significantly related to the ratio in the original models, $\tau = .40$, $p < .001$ (Kendall's tau). One assumption could be that the participants were not motivated to figure out the precise window-wall ratio in the apartment exploration scenario. This experiment is scheduled to include 24 empirical trials. Since the conducting is currently not completed, only the preliminary results of the first 8 participants are reported in this paper.

3.3   Comparison of the Experiments

Using the extended interface providing supplementary information about the windows by sonification, some participants achieve better performance in floor plan sketching (Fig. 4). The average of sketch production scores increased from 2.91 to 3.55, $t(110)=$ 2.99, $p < .01$. This improvement mainly results from better recognition of L-shapes in local and global forms. The percentage of participants who recognized the L-shape in floor plan #3 and #4 increased from 45 to 87.5, and from 25 to 37.5. With respect to the recognition of the global L-shapedness, all of the eight participants who explored with sonification can tell the global L-shape of apartment #2, whereas 75 percent succeeded in recognizing the L-shapedness of #4, which is improved from 50 percent. Furthermore, when the 'windows' are placed on the concave edges of the global L-shape, it seems to be very evident clues over the global shape for the participants. All participants who explored floor plan #4a were able to tell the global L-shape, but only 50 percent with #4b. The scores of the size-ordering task in the Experiment 1 (*Mean* = 5.11, *SE* = 0.13) did not differ significantly from those of Experiment 2 (*Mean* = 5.53, *SE* = 0.13), $t(110)= 1.86, p > .05$.

With this result, we claim that the employment of sonification provides the users with richer information without obvious negative side effects detected.

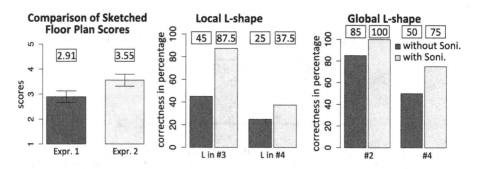

Fig. 4. Comparison between interfaces without sonification and with sonification

4   Discussion and Future Work

Both experiments show that comprehensive knowledge of small-scale apartments could be acquired using the haptic-audio interface. When the interface was augmented with sonification, users were able to acquire supplementary information about windows and show additional improvement in two evaluation tasks. In order to attain more complete and convincing results, additional trials of Experiment 2 are currently ongoing.

Although the recognition of L-shapedness has been improved in the second experiment, systematic analyses of L-shape-phenomena are pending. The proportion of the two edges of the concave corners seems to be one parameter affecting users' perception and cognition. The concave-edge-proportion (CEP) of the L-shaped room in floor plan #3 is 3, while that of the one in floor plan #4 is 5.5. An assumption of the authors is that the closer the value of CEP to 1 is, the easier it is for the users to recognize the inside corner (Fig.5 (a) & (b)). A qualitative investigation of the influence from CEP is desired. Another relevant factor affecting local L-shape recognition seems to consider the proportions between the area of one *L-branch-extensions* and the other *L-branch*, which is the ratio of area, where is shadowed over not shadowed (Fig.5 (c)). In order to figure out the relevant determining parameters affecting perception and cognition of L-shaped rooms using a haptic-audio interface, a systematic study is in preparation.

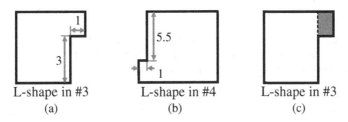

L-shape in #3   L-shape in #4   L-shape in #3
    (a)   (b)   (c)

Fig. 5. Depictions for two L-shaped areas employed in the experiment

The results of global L-shape confirm the argument by Tversky that people do have inference ability based on the spatial information comprehended [17]. Such properties as the layout of the apartment and window configuration are supposed to affect the recognition of the global shape. When different rooms extend the apartment from the hallway towards obviously different directions, which is the case with floor plan #2, or when participants are provided with some clues of the concave edge of the entire global shape, such as the window configuration in floor plan #4a in Fig. 2, participants are more likely to recognize of the correct global shape. More specific research on the interaction of floor plan exploration and reasoning based on general knowledge about apartments and their standard layouts are planned for the future.

Acknowledgement. The research reported in this paper has been partially supported by DFG (German Science Foundation) in the international research training group "Cross-modal Interaction in Natural and Artificial Cognitive Systems" (CINACS, IRTG 1247). The writing of this paper would have not been possible without the excellent comments from Kris Lohmann. We thank the anonymous reviewers for their helpful comments and suggestions.

References

1. Bradley, J.V.: Complete Counterbalancing of Immediate Sequential Effects in Latin Squares Design. Journal of the American Statistical Association 53, 525–528 (1958)
2. Espinosa, M.A., Ungar, S., Ochaita, E., Blades, M., Spencer, C.: Comparing Methods for Introducing Blind and Visually Impaired People to Unfamiliar Urban Environments. Journal of Environmental Psychology 18, 277–287 (1998)

3. Habel, C., Kerzel, M., Lohmann, K.: Verbal Assistance in Tactile-Map Explorations: A case for visual representations and reasoning. In: Proceedings of AAAI Workshop on Visual Representations and Reasoning (2010)
4. Ishikawa, T., Nakata, S., Asami, Y.: Perception and Conceptualization of House Floor Plans: An Experimental Analysis. Environment and Behavior 43, 233–251 (2011)
5. Lahav, O., Mioduser, D.: Haptic-feedback Support for Cognitive Mapping of Unknown Spaces by People who are Blind. Intern. J. Human-Computer Studies 66, 23–35 (2008)
6. Lohmann, K., Eschenbach, C., Habel, C.: Linking Spatial Haptic Perception to Linguistic Representations: Assisting Utterances for Tactile-Map Explorations. In: Egenhofer, M., Giudice, N., Moratz, R., Worboys, M. (eds.) COSIT 2011. LNCS, vol. 6899, pp. 328–349. Springer, Heidelberg (2011)
7. Lohmann, K., Habel, C.: Extended Verbal Assistance Facilitates Knowledge Acquisition of Virtual Tactile Maps. In: Schill, K., Stachniss, C., Uttal, D. (eds.) Spatial Cognition 2012. LNCS (LNAI), vol. 7463, pp. 299–318. Springer, Heidelberg (2012)
8. Loomis, J., Klatzky, R., Lederman, S.: Similarity of Tactual and Visual Picture Recognition with Limited Field of View. Perception 20, 167–177 (1991)
9. Magnusson, C., Rassmus-Gröhn, K.: A Virtual Traffic Environment for People with Visual Impairments. Visual Impairment Research 7, 1–12 (2005)
10. McGookin, D., Brewster, S., Priego, P.: Audio Bubbles: Employing Non-speech Audio to Support Tourist Wayfinding. In: Altinsoy, M.E., Jekosch, U., Brewster, S. (eds.) HAID 2009. LNCS, vol. 5763, pp. 41–50. Springer, Heidelberg (2009)
11. Nees, M.A., Walker, B.N.: Auditory Interfaces and Sonification. In: Stephanidis, C. (ed.) The Universal Access Handbook, pp. 507–521. CRC Press, New York (2009)
12. Paneels, S., Roberts, J.C.: Review of Designs for Haptic Data Visualization. IEEE Transactions on Haptics 3, 119–137 (2010)
13. Petrie, H., King, N., Burn, A., Pavan, P.: Providing Interactive Access to Architectural Floorplans for Blind People. British Journal of Visual Impairment 24, 4–11 (2006)
14. Rassmus-Gröhn, K.: User Centered Design of Non-Visual Audio-Haptics. Doctoral Thesis, Certec, Lund University 2 (2008)
15. Sjöström, C., Danielsson, H., Magnusson, C., Rassmus-Gröhn, K.: Phantom-based haptic line graphics for blind persons. Visual Impairment Research 5, 13–32 (2003)
16. Soechting, J.F., Flanders, M.: Multiple Factors Underlying Haptic Perception of Length and Orientation. IEEE Transactions on Haptics 4, 263–272 (2011)
17. Tversky, B.: Cognitive Maps, Cognitive Collages, and Spatial Mental Models. In: Frank, A., Campari, I. (eds.) COSIT 1993. LNCS, vol. 716, pp. 14–24. Springer, Heidelberg (1993)
18. Wang, Z., Li, B., Hedgpeth, T., Haven, T.: Instant Tactile-audio Map: Enabling Access to Digital Maps for People with Visual Impairment. In: Proceedings of 11th SIGACCESS Conference on Computers and Accessibility, pp. 43–50. ACM, Pittsburg (2009)
19. Yu, J., Habel, C.: Accuracy Scores of Sketched Floor Plans. Technical Report, Department of Informatics, University of Hamburg, Germany (2012)
20. Zeng, L., Weber, G.: Audio-Haptic Browser for a Geographical Information System. In: Miesenberger, K., Klaus, J., Zagler, W., Karshmer, A. (eds.) ICCHP 2010, Part II. LNCS, vol. 6180, pp. 466–473. Springer, Heidelberg (2010)

Mobile Haptic Technology Development through Artistic Exploration

David Cuartielles[1], Andreas Göransson[2], Tony Olsson[2], and Ståle Stenslie[3]

[1] Medea, Malmö University, Sweden
david.cuartielles@mah.se
[2] K3 - Malmö University, Sweden
{andreas.goransson,tony.olsson}@mah.se
[3] Faculty of Humanities, Aalborg University, Denmark
stenslie@hum.aau.dk

Abstract. This paper investigates how artistic explorations can be useful for the development of mobile haptic technology. It presents an alternative framework of design for wearable haptics that contributes to the building of haptic communities outside specialized research contexts. The paper also presents our various wearable haptic systems for mobile computing capable of producing high-order tactile percepts. Our practice based approach suggests a design framework that can be applied to create advanced haptic stimulations/situations for physically embodied interaction in real-world settings.

Keywords: Applied haptics, wearables, bodysuit, haptic and embodied interaction, haptic resolution, Arduino, Android, mobile haptic systems, online haptics editor.

1   Introduction

This paper presents several of our artistic developments using mobile haptic technology with multiple tactile outputs (16+). These represent low cost, open-source haptic systems that use off the shelf components. Our approach intends to act as toolsets for designers working with haptic systems that create emotional and immersive haptic experiences. Rather than developing customized systems aimed at specific tasks or purposes we have made a set of "modules" that are tied together with a shared communication protocol. This approach allows for quick high-fidelity prototype development and faster, simplified iterations of the design. Since our projects are primarily based on standard components, they can be developed at a low start-up cost and propagate reusability.

Our projects have progressed in a chain of iterated design processes where the hardware and the conceptual components have affected each other. The conceptual content part of the system is based on an experimental media art approach where the goal is to create a multisensory, immersive and embodied experience system centered on an open exploration of a *poetics of touch*. The term embodiment is here understood as a combination of both a physical presence in the world and a social embedding in a

C. Magnusson, D. Szymczak, and S. Brewster (Eds.): HAID 2012, LNCS 7468, pp. 31–40, 2012.

web of practices and purposes [1]. The resulting systems have been successfully tried at several usability tests during public art events in Norway, Sweden, Denmark and Slovenia.

1.1   Haptic Systems History

In history the concept of haptic communication through cutaneous touch can be traced back to Giovanni Battista della Porta who in 1558 described the sympathetic telegraph [2]. His proposal was to use magnetism to send and receive the same message over distance, encrypting and decrypting messages by tapping on to the body of two users. This rather imaginative device has never been built, but the concept represents an interesting first approach towards personal, direct and embodied corporal connectivity.

Other early concepts involving touch was Edison's *'Telephonoscope'* [3] which preconceived a telepresence system much like the later videoconferencing systems of today. An important inspiration for telepresence is the notion of being present at the other end of the communication line, as if one was physically present, sensing and interacting with one's own body.

One early important work on tactile interface technology was Bach-y-Rita's first 'tactile display' built in the 1960s [4]. A 20-by-20 array of metal rods in the back of chair were wired to act as the pixels of a screen and functioned much like an electronic Braille writer continuously raising and lowering 'dots' recognizable by the tactile senses. With this tactile display people sitting in the chairs could identify 'pictures' as they were poked into their backs. In effect this demonstrates cross modal perception, allowing us to see images with our sense of touch [5].

Creating a sense of tactile immersion through tactile manipulation of the senses is still difficult to invoke. Current haptic systems within areas such as telemedicine, telerobotics, CAD/CAM and virtual reality are primarily desktop based using technologies such as the PHANToM[1] (Personal HAptic iNTerface Mechanism) [5] and haptic gloves [6]. Most haptic interaction systems are based on a desktop paradigm [7]. This also goes for high resolution wearable displays such as the Tactile Torso Displays [8]. In our world of emerging smartphone- and mobile computing for users on the move, we foresee the need of wearable systems with a higher degree of mobility.

1.2   Towards Mobile and Wearable Haptic Systems

Today there exist no standard or commercially available systems for complex, high resolution haptic interfaces dedicated to mobile and wearable use. At the same time users are adapting to simple haptic systems such as vibrating screens and mobile phones, indicating both the growing need and possibility for somatosensory and haptic systems in communications and experience design. In later years wearable computing has become an extension of ubiquitous computing. This post-desktop, user-centric paradigm of human-computer-interaction focuses on embedding computational power

---

[1] http://www.sensable.com/products-haptic-devices.htm accessed on June 7, 2012.

seamlessly in everyday objects [9]. York also refers to it as machine fitting into the human environment [10]. By fitting haptic technology onto and into our bodies we can provide mobile users with information that was previously unavailable [11], one example being site-specific information and sensing related to users position (GPS) and orientation. For example the *'FeelSpace'* belt enables its user to feel his/her orientation in space via vibrotactile stimulation [12]. Such wearable systems are within a wearer's intimacy zone and therefore also have the potential to provide novel and highly expressive forms of interactions. An early example of wearable, haptic bodysuits, albeit attached to desktop computers, is the *'cyberSM'* system from 1993 [13] that connects two users over the internet allowing them to see, hear and touch each other.

One of the first mobile and telehaptic art projects was the *'Mobile Feelings'* project (2002-03) by Christa Sommerer & Laurent Mignonneau [14]. Here two users each held an egg shaped communication interface that let the users exchange heartbeats. The haptic effect was created with only one vibratory output, but still let users 'feel a strong sensation of bodily connection' [15]. They also note that 'the sense of touch still remains one of our most private sensation for which we still lack a concise language to describe'. However, as a language of touch appears contingent on haptic resolution[2] [13], it is likely that the minimal haptic resolution of one vibrator influenced the lack of haptic expressivity.

The *'Hug Shirt'* by the CuteCircuit company [16] attempts to construct haptic communication for simple, personal messages between users wearing what appears to be a normal looking shirt. The shirt transmits 'hugs' to another, similar shirt via a Bluetooth and Java enabled telephone device. The stimulus resembling a hug is produced by vibrotactile stimulation. Although scarcely described the shirt apparently has a haptic resolution of 10+ effectors. The company has worked on developing a taxonomy of hugs, but its effects are unclear. Another similar project is the *'Huggy Pyjamas'* by Cheok [17] that exchanges hugs through pneumatic actuators, allowing stronger sensations, but on the cost of wearability.

Thecla Schiphorst has worked on developing 'Semantics of Caress' [18] that investigates how the meaning of touch can be applied to tactile interaction. This system represents touch and movement as something meaningful, contributing to quality sharing. Having identified intrinsic values of haptic communication in systems with relatively low haptic resolution, one of our research questions has been how this can be translated into functioning, wearable systems that produce a greater degree of tactile immersion? High fidelity haptics implies a haptic resolution of 90+ effectors/ actuators [13].

Usability issues such as weight, volume and power consumption poses a serious challenge to future system designs of wearable, mobile haptic systems. Lindeman et al.'s research [19] on full-body haptic feedback through applications made with their *'TactaVest'* haptic feedback system attempts to complete the user's sense of tactile immersion in a VR-based environment. The resolution of the early *TactaVest* physically confirms the haptic vision [5] experienced through VR. However, with only 8+ vibrotactile effectors it does not appear to have a high enough haptic resolution to provide a sense of sensory immersion on its own.

---

[2] As the number of stimulators over surface of stimulation.

2   Artistic Research Methodology

The development of our haptic system has followed the path of affective interaction design where key aspects of the process are to effect emotional responses in the target user [20]. Emotional experiences do not solely reside in our minds or brains. They are experienced throughout our whole bodies [21]. Emotions have a crucial role in the human ability to understand and learn new things. Objects that are aesthetically pleasing appear to the user to be more effective by virtue of their sensual appeal [22].

Our research into affective haptics is grounded theoretically on practiced-based artistic research that is formed by the practice of making art [23]. Such artistically guided research is integrated in our projects through the construction of different practical-aesthetical experiments. Our various projects represent empirical research through testing prototypes of mobile, haptic interfaces. The advantages of building prototypes are many [24]. First of all it facilitates testing conditions that are not covered by established principles of design. Second, it provides an evaluation of a first concept for user interface as well as giving quick feedback from the user(s). Drawbacks include the temporary and limited experiential construction of prototypes. The scope of our prototypes has been to cover specific and aesthetically relevant aspects of technologically produced touch.

All our experiments have an open, explorative character, addressing the affective dimensions of haptic experience. How is this useful in scientific contexts? According to Schön, artistic works can be seen to represent knowledge, and the way the artist makes them reflects artistic methods [25]. We see making artworks as an integral part in building systematic knowledge about the use and application of haptic experiences. Our combination of affective interaction design approach with artistic exploration attempts to provoke emotional experiences in the user target group to reveal areas of problems throughout the different iterations of the hardware design.

Throughout our projects we have systematically applied a combination of the following methods: i) artistic practice-based research, ii) user interviews and iii) user observation. These were applied as tools to systematically create knowledge relevant to our goal of gaining insight and knowledge about haptic stimulus in mobile settings. The complex and multifaceted character of practical-aesthetical experiments demands bricolaged and interdisciplinary methods, therefore the use of 'hybrid methodology' is also suitable to describe our research

2.1   First Generation Mobile Haptics

Our first collaborative project, World Ripple, used GPS coordinates and satellite based navigation to create 'immaterial sculptures placed in the open outdoor landscape. The sculptures are either location based events, a kind of haptic theatre, or dynamic (data) structures moving, changing, developing their dimensions and properties over time' [26]. Users wore a bodysuit controlled by a GPS enabled laptop which connected to a micro-controller board and a custom made extension board called *'the dusk'* made for controlling the 64 coin-shaped vibrators inside the bodysuit. The bodysuit is worn underneath the ordinary clothing and the portable, sensor- and GPS based system is carried in a shoulder bag together with a laptop computer which controlled the entire system.

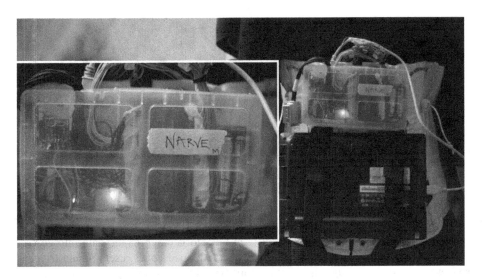

Fig. 1. Controller box with DUSK board (64 actuators) for BlindTheatre Bodysuit

The next iteration of the system was named 'The Blind Theatre' and turned the body into the stage of a somatic theatre (Fig. 1 and 2). It was performed indoors in 2009 at the Norwegian National Theatre in Oslo[3]. Users experienced an audio-haptic story while walking blindfolded around in the theatre. They reported high-order tactile percepts such as stroking, rubbing and caressing [27].

Fig. 2. The bodysuit for the Blind Theater. The haptic suit had two functional layers, one inner corsette and an outer, looser-fit cape.

---

[3] The blind theater project. http://blindtheater.wordpress.com

2.2   Second Generation Mobile Haptics

The third iteration of the design replaced the laptop with the use of smartphones. This increased both comfort and maneuverability due to the smartphones weight and small form factor.

Fig. 3. The Psychoplastic bodysuit during use in Ljubljana 2010

Much like World Ripple this system used GPS to geotagg haptic data into zones defined by spatial coordinates. When entering predefined zones, users would trigger and sense the space through different combinations of vibrotactile patterns and sound (voice).

The phone both acted as GPS receiver and also ran the application controlling the vibrotactile outputs. The data was sent via Bluetooth to a custom made hardware named "Leaf" which consisted of a communication and control board extending into 5 boards shaped like flower leafs where each board controlled 16 vibrating motors, totaling 80 high-resolution actuators.

2.3   The Sense Memory Experiment

In the next Sense Memory experiment (2011) we simplified the system in order to experiment with an outdoor theatre involving multiple users. Constraints were cost and reliability. Using the new Arduino Mega board to Android system, the body suit contained only 16 high-resolution actuators. Although the haptic resolution was significantly lower, it simplified the first iteration of development and allowed us to prototype new hardware solutions within hours, focusing on maximizing the haptic effects outputs and design of haptic patterns. This also simplified the construction of the bodysuit, allowing us to – if needed – rapidly produce multiple suits.

Shaped as a cape (Fig. 4) the final bodysuit was designed for all-weather, outdoor use. Also here the user experienced invisible 'sculptures' by walking around in selected areas. New sets of haptic sculptures/expressions were geo-tagged onto 30+ zones placed around the square. Once the user enters one of the invisible geographic zones the sculptures came alive inside the cape as a combination of binaural sounds and vibrotactile patterns. Every zone contained different words and poetic expressions about emptiness in combination with unique haptic patterns. Here the user's walk formed combinations of touch and words into a unique somatosensory story.

Fig. 4. The Sense Memory Cape during the Malmö test

2.4   User Observation and Analysis

As part of our artistic research user feedback were collected through conducting in-formal interviews with several participants throughout all the iterations of the system. In combination with our own observations we present the following analytical results:

1. Immersive closure of space: Walking around in the public square during normal daytime activities, users reported they were mindful of it beforehand, but once in-side one of the suit they quickly immersed into the experience and forgot about possible onlookers. This indicates a closure of space, strengthening users' sense of an intimate, personal and 'inner' experience.
2. Multimodal strengthening of senses indicating the affective roles of haptics and audio in interaction: the cross-modal combination of sound and touch was expe-rienced as intermingled, intertwined into a mutual strengthening of stimulus. Most users reported focusing mainly on the sound heard and that this appeared as the strongest stimulus. However, they also commented that the touches experienced made them stay longer, thus intensifying the overall sensation of body and space.
3. Increase of spatial awareness: a higher degree of spatial awareness was both ob-served and reported. Users wearing one of the systems noticeably changed their movement in space, becoming more aware of how they were moving to find both new and previous zones of experience.
4. Behavioral change: as users were free to move around in the open space we possi-bly expected a systematic, grid like search for the various interactive areas. How-ever, once they entered the first interactive area they tended to move slowly before stopping. Thereafter they were observed to move in what can be described as an ir-regular, search like manner, moving back and forth, turning back to previous zones. The quick adaptation to new movement and behavior indicates how easily users can adapt to haptic technologies.

2.5   Discussion

There are both benefits and problems with using an artistic exploration approach to the development of a wearable haptic system. Benefits compared to a traditional engineering approach that would focus on low level powering issues, long battery lives, or similar, is the artistic based strengthening of focus on the experiential dimension and user experience. Haptic and content related issues so become much more apparent in the early stages of development. In this way we can be more effective in creating valuable user experiences in faster design iterations. Such findings include positioning and repositioning of vibrotactile effectors in relation to sound and sequencing of haptic patterns. Focusing on users' sense of embodiment and immersion we found that anything less than 64 high-resolution haptic actuators seem to reduce the strength of the experience. When compared to other projects using higher densities of high resolution, vibrotactile stimulation such as Erotogod [13] a preferable number for a full bodysuit covering most parts of the body would be 90+.

One major challenge is how to develop and design haptic patterns that allow for high-order tactile percepts. Although not treated specifically here, our projects have designed iterations of haptic editors that facilitate rapid coding and testing of advanced haptic patterns. In combination with our wide range of body suit designs this allows for optimal actuator placement and combinations on the body.

Other challenges connected to the use of an artistic exploration approach relate to the evaluation of user feedback. In the nature of interactive art projects, the user becomes an integral part of the emotional experience they are evaluating. Though observations were made on changes in behavioral patterns during tests, assuring their scientific relevance is difficult since the users could not, in most cases, confirm or deny these changes as they were both performing an art project and at the same time being the actual art piece.

3   Conclusion and Future Developments

This paper contributes to i) the construction of functional, wearable and haptic experience systems and ii) the discourse of how actual embodiment is experienced within human computer interaction. The combination of i) hardware development and ii) conceptual, aesthetical work has greatly helped us develop new scenarios and novel approaches to the field of haptics. Our field tests show how geotagging haptic experiences greatly affects the users embodied experiences such as sense of place. Another outcome from our experiments is the suggestion that the experience of full body haptic immersion need a haptic resolution of 90+ effectors. There are many improvements to be made and future developments need to include high resolution and wearable prototypes capable of producing advanced haptic experiences for users on the move. Another aim is setting up a more rigid frame work for the evaluation of the artistic exploration approach to strengthen the academic relevance of the highly subjective results such artworks produce.

References

1. Dourish, P.: Where the action is: The Foundations of Embodied Interaction. The MIT Press, Cambridge (2001)
2. Barnouw, E.: Mass communication: television, radio, film, press: the media and their practice in the United States of America. Rinehart, New York (1956)
3. Grau, O.: Virtual Art – From Illusion to Immersion. The MIT Press, Cambridge (2004)
4. Zielinski, S.: Archäologie der Medien. Rowohlt Taschenbuch Verlag (2002)
5. Paterson, M.: The Senses of Touch: Haptics, Affects and Technologies. Berg, Oxford (2007)
6. Fong, B., Fong, A.C.M., Li, C.K.: Telemedicine Technologies: Information Technologies in Medicine and Telehealth. John Wiley & Sons, West Sussex (2011)
7. Dominjon, L., Perret, J., Lécuyer, A.: Novel devices and interaction techniques for human-scale haptics. The Visual Computer 23, 257–266 (2007)
8. Van Veen, H.A.H.C., Van Erp, J.B.F.: Providing Directional Information with Tactile Torso Displays. Presented at Eurohaptics 2003 (2003)
9. Weiser, M.: The computer for the 21st century. ACM SIGMOBILE Mobile Computing and Communications Review 3, 3–11 (1991)
10. York, J., Pendharkar, P.C.: Human-computer interaction issues for mobile computing in a variable work context. International Journal of Human-Computer Studies 60, 771–797 (2004)
11. Marion, A., Heinsen, E., Chin, R., Helmso, B.: Wrist instrument opens new dimension in personal information. Hewlett-Packard Journal (1977)
12. Nagel, S.K., Carl, C., Kringe, T., Märtin, R., König, P.: Beyond sensory substitution - learning the sixth sense. Journal of Neural Engineering 2, 13–26 (2005)
13. Stenslie, S.: Virtual Touch – A study of the user and experience of touch in artistic, multimodal and computer-based environments. Oslo School of Architecture and Design, Oslo (2010)
14. Sommerer, C., Mignonneau, L.: Mobile Feelings –wireless communication of heartbeat and breath for mobile art. In: Proceedings of The 14th International Conference on Artificial Reality and Telexistence, ICAT (2004)
15. Ibid (Sommerer & Mignonneau, 2004)
16. Seymour, S.: Fashionable Technology. Springer, Vienna (2001)
17. Cheok, A.D.: Art and Technology of Entertainment Computing and Communication. Springer, London (2010)
18. Schiphorst, T.: soft(n): Toward a Somaesthetics of Touch. In: Proc. of the 27th International Conference Extended Abstracts on Human Factors in Computing Systems, pp. 2427–2438. ACM, Boston (2009)
19. Lindeman, R.W., Page, R., Yanagida, Y., Sibert, J.L.: Towards Full-Body Haptic Feedback: The Design and Deployment of a Spatialized Vibrotactile Feedback System. In: Proc. of ACM Virtual Reality Software and Technology (VRST), Hong Kong, China, pp. 146–149 (2004)
20. Picard, R.W.: Affective Computing. MIT Press, Cambridge (1997)
21. Davidson, R.J., Scherer, K.R., Goldsmith, H.H.: Handbook of Affective Sciences. Oxford University Press, New York (2002)
22. Norman, D.: Emotional Design. Basic Books, New York (2005)

23. Biggs, M., Karlsson, H.: The Routledge Companion to Research in the Arts, p. 126. Taylor & Francis (2010)
24. Stary, C.: Interaktive Systeme. Software Entwicklung und Software-Ergonomie. Vieweg Informatik/Wirtschaftsinformatik (1996)
25. Schön, D.: The Reflective Practitioner. Basic Books, New York (1983)
26. World Ripple, http://www.stenslie.net/?page_id=85
27. Gibson, J.: The senses considered as perceptual systems. Houghton Mifflin, Boston (1966)

Improving Cyclists Training
with Tactile Feedback on Feet

Dominik Bial[1], Thorsten Appelmann[1], Enrico Rukzio[2], and Albrecht Schmidt[3]

[1] Paluno – The Ruhr Institute for Software Technology, University of Duisburg-Essen,
Gerlingstraße 16, 45127 Essen, Germany
Dominik.Bial@paluno.uni-due.de, Thorsten.Appelmann@uni-due.de
[2] Institute for Media Informatics, Ulm University,
James-Franck-Ring, 89081 Ulm, Germany
enrico.rukzio@uni-ulm.de
[3] SimTech & VIS, University of Stuttgart,
Pfaffenwaldring 5a, 70569 Stuttgart, Germany
Albrecht.Schmidt@vis.uni-stuttgart.de

Abstract. This paper explores how tactile feedback can support cyclist in order to fulfill user-defined training programs. Therefore, actuators are integrated in cyclists' shoes. The rhythm the cyclist should pedal is communicated via tactile feedback so that the heart rate is kept in an interval which is, for example, optimal for increasing stamina. After a preliminary study, which was used to gather the optimal position for the actuators on feet, a working prototype of such a system was developed. This prototype was tested in a preliminary study by two participants in the wild. They were able to understand the communicated tactile feedback, enjoyed using our system and stated that they could imagine using such a system regularly. This indicates that communicating tactile feedback via the user's feet is another application domain where vibration signals can be of high benefit and can be used to communicate information to the user as audio or visual information are not appropriate.

Keywords: human computer interaction, tactile feedback, actuators, traffic, mobile phone, cyclists, prototype.

1   Introduction

Our feet are an elementary part in our everyday life and are necessary during activities such as cycling, driving motorcars and motorcycles. Nevertheless, their tasks are rather limited to, for example, braking and pedaling, and are very rarely used for human-computer-interaction. The usage of tactile feedback broadens the spectrum of communication channels beside the obvious visual and audio channels. Moreover, research shows that tactile feedback is even less intrusive and distractive [2].Tactile feedback on feet promises to be beneficial for users especially if other parts of the body are already engaged. Moreover, there are many nerve ends in the human foot so that it is an extremely sensitive body part regarding vibration signals. This can be of special interest for motorcyclists, drivers and cyclists.

C. Magnusson, D. Szymczak, and S. Brewster (Eds.): HAID 2012, LNCS 7468, pp. 41–50, 2012.
© Springer-Verlag Berlin Heidelberg 2012

Out of this mentioned group we focused on cyclists to gather information about the feasibility to communicate information via tactile feedback on the human foot. First, an initial user study was conducted to test suitable positions and arrangements for actuators. Then, a prototype was designed to support individual training programs of cyclists based on their heart rate. A vibration based pulse generator was developed to find out about the feasibility of such a system. Vibration signals were sent to a cyclist telling which pedal rhythm to keep so that a certain heart rate interval is not exceeded or underrun. Two participants were asked to test the prototype.

Fig. 1. Participant testing the final prototype

This paper starts with an overview over related work in section 2, section 3 discusses the overall concept and section 4 different components of the prototype while section 5 introduces results from a user study testing the configuration of the tactile feedback being provided. This study was used to determine the best position and arrangement of the actuators on feet. Section 6 reports on results gathered with the help of participants who tested the prototype in the wild.

2   Related Work

Current research shows that tactile pulses are automatically decoded from anatomical into external coordinates, as in the paper of Roeder et al. [11] who compared the response time of congenitally blind and late blind with sighted humans. The participants had to wear headphones and to press a left or right response key depending on the acoustical signal bursts presented from either the left or right loudspeaker.

Within this context one could distinguish the follow two research strands: firstly, tactile feedback as navigational aid, secondly, tactile feedback in the health and sports domain. In the field of supporting navigation several approaches can be found. Bial et al. investigated the recognition rate of actuators fixed in two motorcyclists' gloves [1]. The aim was to find suitable positions of actuators for a navigation prototype based on tactile feedback. The Tactile Wayfinder is a prototype consisting of six actuators placed around a belt, which can assist users by means of directed impulses [4].

Poppinga et al. installed tactile motors in the handlebar of a bike to support the navigation of cyclists by varying the signal strength on the handles [10]. By combining tactile feedback in a steering wheel with a navigation device Kern et al. examined the opportunity to communicate directions through vibration pulses [7]. A similar approach was pursued by Hogema et al. who placed actuators in a driving seat [6]. The works mentioned before show the benefit of tactile feedback in traffic. Besides that, there is further information which could be communicated to road users than navigation. For example, giving hints about approaching cars and training performance while cycling seems to be promising.

In the field of health and sports domain Spelmezan et al. examined the use of actuators for learning complex movement sequences, such as snowboarding [12]. Therefore, a bodysuit equipped with several actuators was developed which communicated how to move the body best while snowboarding. A corresponding study showed that the participants equipped with actuators performed equally well compared to participants who received instructions given by a trainer. Music-touch Shoes are dancing shoes with actuators in a sole [13]. This shall help deaf people to *feel* music and allow them to move to its beat. Lylykangas et al. [10] used tactile feedback to regulate behaviour of users. Tactile signals varied in frequency, modulation and waveform to distinguish various information. The results indicate that tactile feedback can be used to guide users without overloading their visual and auditory channels. Additionally, vibration feedback can be accompanied by other haptic feedback as shown by Jirattigalachote et al [8]. Jirattigalachote et al. conducted a study to analyze the perception of tactile feedback in combination with a haptic feedback device called virtual pebble. This work suggests combining haptic feedback devices with vibration patterns which shall be addressed in future work.

3   Concept

Tactile feedback can be used to communicate warnings, threats or simply to give hints. To test the feasibility of tactile feedback under real conditions we imagine an application which supports cyclists in their training. In a gym, typically, the heart rate is measured to compute the energy consumption, to give hints to the user or to control the speed or resistance. Pulse watches like the POLAR heart rate monitor watches[1] allow users to control the current pulse visually and some devices provide audio feedback when a certain hart rate is reached. Tactile feedback provides distinct advantages when running or cycling as the usage of visual or audio information might distract the users from the environment, other people and the surrounding traffic.

Our concept is different from previous approaches as the tactile feedback is provided via the user's feet through where the user doesn't have to wear a potentially disturbing wirstlets or gloves. Tactile feedback could be provided by the handles as well when the user is cycling but the handles are not always touched and tactile feedback is significantly reduced when the user wears gloves. Tactile shoes don't suffer from those disadvantages.

---

[1] http://www.polarusa.com/us-en/products/get_active/
running_multisport/RS100

Our system communicates various information such as the frequency with which the user should pedal or run (e.g. in order to achieve a certain hart rate) and whether she should change gears when cycling. The frequency in which the user should pedal or run is communicated by alternating tactile feedback on the left and right foot. Such information can't efficiently be communicated by a pulsed watch or the handles. When communicated via boots the user receives the feedback on the foot which should push the pedal forward and should make the next step. Through this a behavior can be simulated that is well-known from various exercise machines (e.g. from cross trainers that change the resistance in relationship to the current hart rate) and allows cyclists or runners an effective training with direct feedback.

We envision that the overall system consists of a pulse watch measuring the users pulse and allows the user to define her training program. The pulse watch communicates then with the tactile shoes in order to give related feedback to the user. Alternatively the user could wear a pulse belt or could control the settings via her mobile phone.

4   Prototype

We developed a prototype in order to test the feasibility of our approach. The prototype consists of six different components which are shown in figure 2.

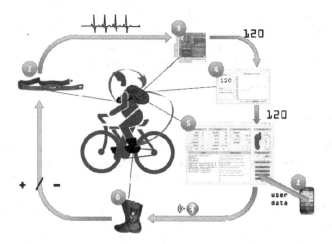

Fig. 2. (2.1) mobile phone as end-user device, (2.2) Polar pulse belt, (2.3) Sparkfun heart rate monitor, (2.4) heart rate recording component, (2.5) actuator controller, (2.6) vibration shoes

An Android application for a mobile phone has been developed to allow the user the configuration and definition of individual training programs (Fig. 2.1). The users can specify their gender, height, age, weight and if they are sporty. Additionally, the users can select the duration for their training as well as one out of four different training programs for cardiovascular training, fat burning, stamina increase and muscle growth. These parameters are used as input to support cyclists' training programs with tactile feedback.

A POLAR sensor needs to be worn by a user to monitor the heart rate (Fig. 2.2). The POLAR Heart Rate Monitor Interface[2] acts as a mediator (Fig. 2.2). It receives data from the sensor and forwards it to a Java Application via a serial connection over USB (Fig. 2.4). This Java application requests the heart rate every second and is responsible for tracking and analyzing this data. A second Java application (Fig. 2.5) is placed on top which controls actuators being attached to the users' feet. In addition, it is responsible for the tactile feedback which shall be used to support the cycling. The actuators are wired to a self-built micro controller board that receives input via Bluetooth and which controls the tactile feedback (Fig. 2.6). This allows controlling the intensity of the actuators in order to communicate different tactile patterns.

The training programs are based on the work by Edward [3] who defines five different zones for the maximum heart rate. Keeping the heart rate in one of these zones has a specific effect on the human body. The health, fat burning, aerobe and anaerobe zones are offered as training zones. The maximum heart rate for a person can be computed with Hills' equations [5]. Hills mainly differentiates between a trained or untrained person in combination with the gender. To find out, if a person is trained or not the body mass index is used. Details are provided in figure 3.

Person	Max. Heart Rate (HR$_{max}$)
Heavily overweighed	200 - (0,5 * Age)
Untrained Woman	209 - (0,7 * Age)
Untrained Man	214 - (0,8 * Age)
Trained Woman	211 - (0,5 * Age)
Trained Man	205 - (0,5 * Age)

Heart Rate Interval	Zone	Wirkung
50 – 60% HR$_{max}$	Health Zone	Improvement of the cardiovascular system
60 – 70% HR$_{max}$	Fat Burning Zone	Fitness improvement and fat burning
70 – 80% HR$_{max}$	Aerobe Zone	Stamina improvement
80 – 90% HR$_{max}$	Anaerobe Zone	Strength and musice development
90 – 100% HR$_{max}$	Warnzone	Risk for untrained persons

Fig. 3. Left: Max heart rate equations by Hills; Right: Edward's training zones [3, 5]

With the help of the parameters which the user specified on the mobile phone the maximum heart rate can be calculated. The maximum heart rate is monitored by our prototype. Clock pulse vibration patterns are used to inform the cyclist to speed up or to slow down.

5   Informing User Preferences

Although the realization of the concept was straight forward, the best positioning of actuators on users' feet was uncertain. We wanted to find out if actuators should be arranged in a line or in an array. Additionally, the position on the foot had to be tested. Therefore, a preliminary user study has been conducted. 12 participants (4 female and 8 male) took part in the study. The oldest participant was 70, the youngest 25 years old. In average the participants were 36.5 years old.

---

[2] http://www.sparkfun.com/products/8661

5.1   Study Design

Actuators which can be found in a Nokia 8800 mobile phone where taken and fixed in a piece of foam (see figure 4). Four actuators were arranged in line while four different ones were placed in a rectangle. These pieces were placed on the ball of the foot, the heel or the ankle. A third order Latin square was used to control the order of the tested configurations for the different positions of the actuators while the arrangement of the actuators was rotated. One participant always started with the actuators in line while another participant always had the array configuration first. Three different pulses were sent which participants had to distinguish. The tested durations were 100ms, 300ms and 800ms. All in all, participants had to delimit 9 signals (3 short, 3 medium and 3 long signals) which were tested with every position and arrangement. This results in a 3x2x3 factorial design: 3 positions (ball, ankle and heel) x 2 arrangements (line and array) x 3 signals (short, medium and long).

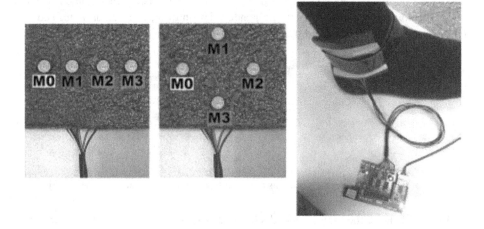

Fig. 4. Actuators arranged in a line and an array - exemplarily positioned at an ankle

5.2   Procedure

After a short introduction into the study, its configurations and the study's purpose participants were asked to take off their shoes and to sit down on a chair with their back to the examiner. The aim was that the participants could not have a glance at the study material like the randomization and notes. Then, the participants were asked to wear headphones during the different runs to make sure that the vibration of the actuators could not be heard and the duration be guessed.

Then, the signals for each configuration were sent to the actuators. The participants had to state if the last signal sent was a short, medium or long one. The examiner noted the correctness or incorrectness. After each configuration a short questionnaire based on [14, 15] was given to the participants which they were asked to fill in. The questionnaire used 5 Level Likert scales to gather information about mental demand, comfort and subjective performance. Finally, participants were briefly interviewed. All in all, the study took roughly 20 minutes for each participant.

5.3   Results

We applied statistic tests to our gathered results. An ANOVA showed that there is no significant effect for the errors participants made during the experiment. However, we do not believe, that there is no difference among the positions and arrangements. In fact, it could be a result of our setting. Participants could fully concentrate on the vibration and were not distracted by their surroundings. Hence, such a system is heavily influenced by real world conditions so that a test in the wild would be necessary.

Additionally, we used questionnaires to ask for the mental demand required for the signal identification, the comfort for wearing the actuators and the participants' self-assessment. However, Friedman ANOVAs did not show any significant effects. Moreover, the mean values and the standard deviation did not differ so that we had to rely on participants' feedback.

At the end of the different runs of the study, the prototype was discussed with the participants and their impressions as well as ideas were noted. The interviews showed that 11 of 12 participants could imagine using tactile feedback on foot while riding a bike or motorcycle. Only one participant mentioned that the vibration felt strange. Additionally, he was concerned about the information content which can be communicated. Therefore, he cannot imagine that such a system could be useful in a real world scenario. The participants mentioned further applications for tactile feedback, for example communicating warnings or navigation.

Asking the participants for their preferred position and arrangement, 6 of the participants would like to have the line arrangement. The other participants had no preference at all. No participant mentioned the array arrangement. 7 participants preferred the actuators to be placed at the balls of the feet, preferably in combination with a line arrangement. Other participants stated to have no preference. This indicates that the best suited position for actuators is the ball in combination with the line arrangement which was used in the final prototype.

6   Preliminary Testing in the Wild

After the preliminary study and the development of the shoes (see figure 5) our prototype from section 4 could be fully implemented. The final prototype sends vibrations pulses to a user telling that her training starts or ends and on which foot to put force on to pedal. We used five different vibration patterns to communicate these actions based on the long and short vibration pulses form the preliminary study with a break of 75 milliseconds in between. When the patterns had to be chosen it was focused on easy differentiation between those.

The training started with three long vibrations signals. Five long signals ended the training. When three short and a long signal are sent the cyclist has to shift up a gear. A long followed up by three short signals lets a user shift down a gear. These patterns are sent to both feet at the same time. A single short signal on the left or the right feet tells on which foot to put force on and helps to establish a certain pedaling frequency to reach a certain hart rate.

We asked two participants (1 male, 36 years and 1 female, 48 years old) to test our design and the vibration patterns under real world conditions to find out the suitability in a realistic context. The participants had to wear the shoes, a POLAR belt and a rucksack where a laptop was placed in. The POLAR heart rate interface was connected to the laptop so that the laptop could process the heart rate data and could control the actuators in the shoes. Additionally, a mobile phone was given to the participants so that they could configure their training program. Two different training programs which took five minutes each were tested by the participants. The tests were carried out on the inner courtyard on a nearby University campus. Figure 1 shows a participant testing the prototype.

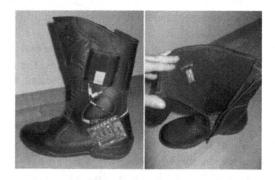

Fig. 5. Shoes providing tactile feedback for cyclists to support their training

A short introduction was given to the participants to inform them about the study and its purpose the participants. The participants were not trained to use the system and had to learn its usage during the study. Afterwards we asked them to configure their training and to cycle in circles in sight of the examiner. The examiner observed the participants and made notes which were used during the followed up interviews. Additionally, the participants' heart rate was tracked.

Exemplarily, the results of a 48 years old participant with a weight of 61kg shall be discussed in detail. Figure 6 shows the tracked data.

The participant chose the fat burning training program and stated to be untrained which resulted in his individual training program. Afterwards, the participant had to keep the rhythm suggested by the vibration signals sent to both feet alternatively.

After the experiment the prototype and the participants' experience were discussed. The participants enjoyed the cycling as well as the experiment. Interestingly, one participant stated that he was even motivated by the vibration to keep on exercising. He liked the idea of having a system which keeps track of the performance as well as improving the personal training. Asking the participant if they would use such a system in traffic and if they think it to be dangerous they said that they do not see any risk.

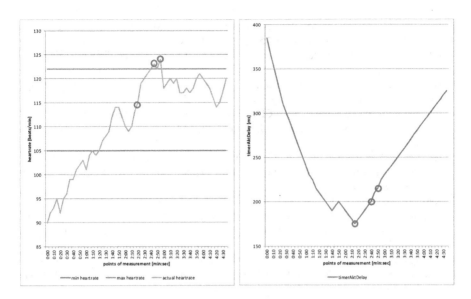

Fig. 6. Exemplary results of one participant

However, participants criticized, that the vibration was too weak so that more powerful actuators should be integrated. Nevertheless, they mentioned that they would like to buy the system and even suggested to apply this concept to further domains like jogging.

7   Conclusion

This paper explores how tactile feedback communicated via the user's feet can be used to communicate pedaling frequency and shifting gears to achieve an optimal training while cycling. First, a user study was conducted to inform the final design of the tactile actuators. Then, a prototype was developed and preliminary user feedback gathered. Two participants tested the prototype in a realistic setting and reported that they were impressed by the system and could imagine using the system regularly. Only a short introduction was necessary before the participants could use the system. This shows that tactile feedback on feet can be of high value for the sports domain. However, this also demonstrates that a further research needs to be conducted and that further vibration hardware and patterns have to be investigated.

References

1. Bial, D., Kern, D., Alt, F., Schmidt, A.: Enhancing Outdoor Navigation Systems through Vibrotactile Feedback. In: Proceedings of the 2011 Annual Conference Extended Abstracts on Human Factors in Computing Systems, CHI EA 2011, pp. 1273–1278. ACM (2011)

2. Brewster, S.A., Brown, L.M.: Tactons: Structured Tactile Messages for non-visual Information Display. In: AUIC 2004, pp. 15–23. Australian Computer Society, Inc. (2004)
3. Edwards, S.: The Heart Rate Monitor Guidebook: To Heart Zone Training. VeloPress (1999)
4. Heuten, W., Henze, N., Boll, S., Pielot, M.: Tactile Wayfinder: A non-visual Support System for Wayfinding. In: Proceedings of the 5th Nordic Conference on Human-Computer Interaction: Building Bridges, NordiCHI 2008, pp. 127–181. ACM (2008)
5. Hills, A.P., Byrne, N.M., Ramage, A.J.: Submaximal Markers of Exercise Intensity. Journal of Sports Sciences 16, 71–76 (1998)
6. Hogema, J.H., De Vries, S.C., Van Erp, J.B.F., Kiefer, R.J.: A Tactile Seat for Direction Coding in Car Driving: Field Evaluation. IEEE Transactions on Acoustics, Speech and Signal Processing Haptics 2, 181–188 (2009)
7. Kern, D., Marshall, P., Hornecker, E., Rogers, Y., Schmidt, A.: Enhancing Navigation Information with Tactile Output Embedded into the Steering Wheel. In: Tokuda, H., Beigl, M., Friday, A., Brush, A.J.B., Tobe, Y. (eds.) Pervasive 2009. LNCS, vol. 5538, pp. 42–58. Springer, Heidelberg (2009)
8. Jirattigalachote, W., Shull, P., Cutkosky, M.: Virtual Pebble: A Haptic State Display for Pedestrians. In: Proceedings of 20th IEEE International Symposium on Robot and Human Interactive Communication, RO-MAN, pp. 401–406. IEEE (2011)
9. Lylykangas, J., Surakka, V., Rantala, J., Raisamo, J., Raisamo, R., Tuulari, E.: Vibrotactile Information for Intuitive Speed Regulation. In: Proceedings of the 23rd British HCI Group Annual Conference on People and Computers: Celebrating People and Technology, BCS-HCI 2009, pp. 112–119. British Computer Society (2009)
10. Poppinga, B., Pielot, M., Boll, S.: Tacticycle: A Tactile Display for Supporting Tourists on a Bicycle Trip. In: Proceedings of the 11th International Conference on Human-Computer Interaction with Mobile Devices and Services, MobileHCI 2009, pp. 41:1–41:4. ACM (2009)
11. Roeder, B., Kusmierek, A., Spence, C., Schicke, T.: Developmental Vision Determines the Reference Frame for the Multisensory Control of Action. In: Proceedings of the National Academy of Sciences, vol. 104, pp. 4753–4758. National Academy of Sciences (2007)
12. Spelmezan, D., Hilgers, A., Borchers, J.: A Language of Tactile Motion Instructions. In: Proceedings of the 11th International Conference on Human-Computer Interaction with Mobile Devices and Services, MobileHCI 2009, pp. 29:1–29:5. ACM (2009)
13. Yao, L., Shi, Y., Chi, H., Ji, X., Ying, F.: Music-Touch Shoes: Vibrotactile Interface for Hearing Impaired Dancers. In: Proceedings of the fourth International Conference on Tangible, Embedded, and Embodied Interaction, TEI 2010, pp. 275–276. ACM (2010)
14. Hart, S.G., Stavenland, L.E.: In Development of NASA-TLX (Task Load Index): Results of empirical and theoretical research. In: Human Mental Workload, pp. 139–183 (1988)
15. Lewis, J.: IBM computer usability satisfaction questionnaires: Psychometric evaluation and instructions for use. International Journal of Human-Computer Interaction 7, 57–78 (1995)

HapticPulse – Reveal Your Heart Rate in Physical Activities

Janko Timmermann[1], Benjamin Poppinga[1], Susanne Boll[2], and Wilko Heuten[1]

[1] OFFIS - Institute for Information Technology, Germany
{Janko.Timmermann,Benjamin.Poppinga,Wilko.Heuten}@offis.de
http://www.offis.de/
[2] University of Oldenburg, Germany
boll@informatik.uni-oldenburg.de
http://medien.informatik.uni-oldenburg.de/

Abstract. The heart rate is an objective parameter indicating the current physical activity. Displaying it to the user will help her or him to gain awareness of the physical load during certain activities. Current systems do not use the sense of touch to display the actual heart rate. Using the sense of touch has been shown to be potentially less distracting than using other senses in certain situations. In this paper we describe a system which displays the heart rate of the user using the sense of touch. We conducted a user study in the field with ten participants to collect qualitative and quantitative data, which serves as a guideline for the future improvement of such systems.

1 Introduction

The heart rate is one of the main parameters representing the level of physical activity. To know the current heart rate is essential for appropriate physical exercises. For example, it is important to keep a specific heart rate range regarding to your training goals [1][10] or even to increase the heart rate variability [2][5] which is a potential marker for health [8]. Measuring the heart rate is very common during sport activities [1].

Experienced runners or cyclists are usually aware of their physical load, their approximate heart rate, and what ranges are suitable for certain exercises. However, people that are new to physical activities have difficulties to understand or feel the necessary load and are often overloaded or underloaded. Such people are for example patients, who are required to reach a particular physical load over a certain time, in order to improve their cardiovascular system after a heart disease. Overstraining can cause further heart problems, while understraining does not have any effect on the improvement of the cardiovascular system. Another example of a user group are people with obesity who need to increase their physical effort. However, in order to keep the motivation of training in the long-term perspective, it is necessary to guide them from the beginning, in particular starting with small exercises, which do not overburden the user. Besides subjective measurements, e.g. asking people how they feel, the heart rate is an objective

C. Magnusson, D. Szymczak, and S. Brewster (Eds.): HAID 2012, LNCS 7468, pp. 51–60, 2012.
© Springer-Verlag Berlin Heidelberg 2012

parameter indicating the current physical activity. Displaying the heart rate to the user will help her or him to gain awareness of physical load during certain activities and enables the user to adjust her or his physical effort according to the recommendations from doctors or training goals.

While many stationary home exercise machines have integrated sensors and displays, there are also watches measuring and displaying the heart rate with the help of a chest belt, which can be used during nearly any outdoor activity. The display usually consists of a number, i.e. the presentation of heartbeats in a minute. Users need to look at the display on demand to perceive this number and to interpret its meaning. Some of these watches also support notification mechanisms with tactile or auditory feedback to alert the user when specified heart rates are exceeded or deceeded.

However, none of these systems are using touch to display the current and actual heart rate, although there has been a lot of research indicating the beneficial use of touch. For example, the sense of touch can handle abstract messages [4] and has shown to be less distracting in certain situations [3][7]. Using it to communicate information to the user enables her or him to get the desired information without using other senses like the visual one by looking at a graphical display. In addition, tactile displays can be perceived without any further interaction of the user. If designed appropriately, they enable users to gain a continuous awareness of the presented information – in our case the heart rate. Furthermore, users can immediately feel the impact of increasing or decreasing the physical load in relation to the heart rate.

In this paper we describe a preliminary system that displays the user's heart rate using the sense of touch. We conducted a field study with 10 users to collect qualitative and quantitative data to serve as a guideline for the future improvement of this system or development of similar systems. The study showed, that users can actually learn about their heart rate by using the HapticPulse and correctly feel it with a certain accuracy. We found out that the device strengthened the awareness of the heart rate. Besides this, we collected interesting qualitative feedback for future improvements for such systems.

2   Related Work

Several approaches are existing that use displaying the heartbeat to create intimacy between two people. Lotan et al. (2007) propose a device "[...] for augmenting intimate or meditative moments between people at a distance [...]". The device has an outline of hands on the surface where the users can place their hands. It is then able to reflect the users' heartbeat or even to simultaneously use two vibration motors to show the heartbeat of the local user and a user of another device [6]. Werner et al. (2008) created a similar approach in which two partners wear rings which enable the wearer to feel the partner's heartbeat with the help of a small vibration motor. Most participants liked the vibrations which felt very similar to a known heartbeat [9].

There are already some commercial products which support the user in measuring the heart rate and in keeping it in defined borders. One example is the *Garmin*

Forerunner 610[1]. Additionally to acoustic signals when the heart rate exceeds certain limits, it can also give tactile feedback in form of a vibration. Apps like *Runkeeper*[2] can track a whole workout and also include heart rate recording, so the users can learn about their heart rate during physical activities.

Brewster et al. (2004) described with tactile icons (Tactons) a method to encode abstract messages with tactile feedback which can for example be used to display information without demanding other senses like sight and hearing [4]. Pielot et al. (2010) used tactons for location encoding and Asif et al (2010) for navigation tasks [3][7]. Both concluded that the tactile information display was equally or less distracting than visual or auditory information.

3   Goals and Approach

Our main goal of this paper is to prove whether users can perceive and interpret a pure tactile representation of the heart rate while walking and running outdoors. We further want to find out if this presentation enables users to adjust their physical activity to reach a previously defined target heart frequency, how accurate they are, and whether there are common deviations between perceived and target heart frequency, depending on the actual physical effort performed by the user. Additionally, we want to collect more qualitative data, such as emotions and suggestions from the users. We are interested in whether the tactile representation is disturbing, distracting, or annoying the user and whether it influences the walking or running rhythms. We also want to find out the subjective impression of how accurate the users reached the target heart rate.

Our approach to find answers to these questions was to develop a simple smart phone application for Android which presents the heart rate by vibration pulses of the smart phone. In this first study, we displayed each heartbeat by one vibration pulse, i.e. making the heart activity directly perceivable for the user, with the intention to provide immediate feedback when the heart frequency changes and to increase the users' experience by enabling them to immerse into the most natural representation of a physical load. Thus, we also avoid the more abstract presentation of heartbeats per minutes, which needs to be interpreted by the user.

4   Field Study

To investigate if the concept of a tactile pulse representing the heartbeat is applicable, we conducted a field study with a strong focus on qualitative feedback.

4.1   Method and Setting

In order to obtain results under realistic conditions, we decided to perform a field study instead of a lab study. After interviewing several medical experts, we

---

[1] http://sites.garmin.com/forerunner610/?lang=en

[2] http://runkeeper.com

provided users with target heart frequencies which should be reached during a physical exercise. To evaluate differences in the perception of different physical load levels, we defined three target heart rates. The three levels were defined as 80, 110, and 140 bpm (beats per minute).

In the beginning of the study the participants received the apparatus and the experimenter explained the procedure of the study. The study consisted of three phases. They differed in the target heart rate which should be reached by the participant. The heart rate was chosen by the application randomly to avoid any learning bias in the study results. Each phase was divided into a learning part and a part with physical activity (e.g. running or walking). During the learning part, the target frequency is mediated to the user. The application plays the target frequency by vibration pulses in the same manner as described above, e.g. if the user should reach a target frequency of 110 beats per minute, the application presents 110 vibration pulses per minute. This allows the user to learn the frequency. We thought this was necessary, because we didn't expect the participants to have any prior experience in measuring heart rates even without beeing physical active. The participants were allowed to do anything during the learning part to get used to the feeling of the displayed target heart rate. The learning part was not limited in time and was ended by the participants themselves. Afterwards, the device switched to the running part. During this part, the measured heart rate of the participant was represented as tactile heartbeat. The participants were asked to try to adjust their walking or running speed so that their heart rate was just as high as the previously learned heart rate. There was no time restriction to reach the target. Once the participants thought they reached it, they had to press a button on the screen and try to keep this target heart rate for two minutes. After these two minutes, the application switched to the learning phase to present the next target frequency.

Questionnaire and Post Interview. Before the study, the participants received a questionnaire and the session ended with a semi-structured interview with some guiding questions. In the questionnaire, we asked the participants for their age, sex, and background knowledge:

1. Do you know about the meaning of the heart rate?
2. Did you use a heart rate monitor before?
3. Do you know about your heart rates at specific loads?

For the open interview, we specified the following guiding questions:

1. How good or bad was the representation of your heart rate?
2. Did the application increase your awareness of your heart rate?
3. To reach the desired heart rate, did you use your feeling or the vibration presented by the app?
4. Did the application distract you?
5. Did the application disturb your walking/running rhythm?

Location. For each session, the experimenter and the participant met at a location chosen by the participant, often an area which is frequently used by runners. The participants were allowed to choose any place, which has no slopes and which provides minimum risk, even when the participant would be distracted by the application.

Participants. We conducted the field study with ten participants: Eight of them male and two female. The age ranged from 21 to 41.

Apparatus. To measure the heart rate, we used a Zephyr HxM[3] heart rate sensor. As smart phone we used the Samsung Galaxy Nexus[4], running Android 4.0. You can see both in *Fig. 1*.

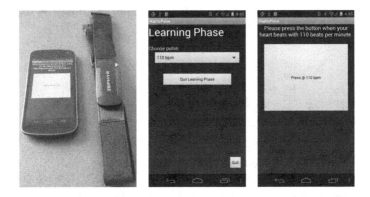

Fig. 1. HapticPulse Apparatus

In order to perform the study, we implemented an application for Android smart phones, which we call *HapticPulse*. The application consists of two screens (see *Fig. 1*): The first screen *Learning Phase* is intended to learn and feel a tactile representation of the heartbeat. The chosen frequency is selected randomly. The user also has the option to manually choose between the three different frequencies. After choosing a frequency it will immediately be presented through tactile pulses. The second screen is intended to instruct the user during the physical exercise (walking and running) and to allow the user to press a button when she or he thinks to have reached that goal. While this screen is shown, the heart rate of the user is constantly represented as tactile pulse. Two minutes after the user indicated that the specified heart frequency is reached, the application switches to the first screen again. The application logs the heart rate reported by the heart rate sensor and any input from the user with time stamps. The participants were asked to carry the device in one of their hands.

---

[3] http://www.zephyr-technology.com/consumer-hxm

[4] http://www.samsung.com/uk/consumer/mobile-devices/smartphones/android/
GT-I9250TSAXEU

4.2   Quantitative Results

Seven participants knew about the meaning of the heart rate. Five had used some kind of heart rate display before, mostly watches. Four participants were even aware of their heart rates during specific activities. These participants were running frequently or had used a heart rate monitor in a fitness center. These data were collected through the questionnaire.

The log files of the application showed that the average duration of the learning parts was 179 seconds (SD 127 seconds) for 80 bpm, 112 seconds (SD 42 seconds) for 110 bpm, and 128 seconds (SD 66 seconds) for 140 bpm. The length of the learning parts seemed not to correlate with the overall performance. The average duration between switching to running mode and subjectively reaching the previous learned heart rate was 134 seconds (SD 89 seconds) for 80 bpm, 46 seconds (SD 47 seconds) for 110 bpm, and 70 seconds (SD 66 seconds) for 140 bpm. The average overall duration of the study, disregarding the explanation and interview, was 17 minutes (SD 4 minutes).

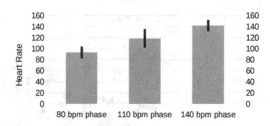

Fig. 2. Average heart rate and standard deviation when the button was pressed

Because we wanted the participants to press a button when they had reached the learned heart rate, it is interesting how accurate they were. As you can see in *Fig. 2*, the average heart rate for the 80 bpm phase was 93 bpm (SD 11 bpm). The average heart rate for the 110 bpm phase was 118 bpm (SD 17 bpm). In comparison with other participants, one participant had a very high value here. His deviation from the desired heart rate was five times higher compared to the other participants. If we eliminate this one measure, the average heart rate would be 114 bpm (SD 7 bpm). The average heart rate for the 140 bpm phase was 142 bpm (SD 10 bpm).

In *Fig. 3* the average heart rates of the participants during the running phases are shown. It reveals that the participants had in average a higher heart rate than the target rate: 93 bpm (SD 11 bpm) in the 80 bpm phase, 122 bpm (SD 16 bpm) in the 110 bpm phase, and 152 bpm (SD 7 bpm) in the 140 bpm phase.

4.3   Qualitative Results

In the interview, we used five guiding questions as mentioned before and gave the opportunity to give feedback.

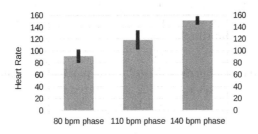

Fig. 3. Average heart rate and standard deviation during running phase

How Good or Bad Was the Representation of your Heart Rate? The participants either answered positive or they did not answer because they had no idea of their heart rate and therefore were not able to classify the representation accuracy. One participant mentioned he would like a live representation and the delay caused him to rate the representation good at constant speeds but bad at changing speeds. It pointed out that he thought the application was rather slow when adapting to a new heart rate, but most of the delay he experienced came from his heart itself. Other participants reported a very direct representation of their heartbeat or that they were only able to feel the delay when standing still. One told us: "Very good. I was able to feel my heart rate very good. I think with an accuracy of 5 beats per minute.". In fact that participant had a deviation of about 6 bpm.

Did the Application Increase Your Awareness of Your Heart Rate? Every participant stated that the application increased their awareness of their heart rate. Some mentioned it would be interesting to get this feedback over a longer period of time to learn about the reactions of the heart to different situations. The advantages of existing heart rate monitors for consumers was mentioned because they show a concrete numerical value. On the other hand one participant mentioned that he sometimes forgets about his heart rate monitor and likes this representation because it is constant and you can not forget about it. One described the feeling as "very intensive" because "you can feel very good how your body reacts". Another one would rather like an application telling him what to do, e.g. "run faster", instead of just showing the pure heart rate.

To Reach the Desired Heart Rate, Did You Use Your Feeling or the Vibration Presented by the App? Most participants mainly used the application to reach the desired heart rate, especially when they had no idea about their heart rate during certain activities. It pointed out that more experience in running led to less usage of the application. One very active participant stated that "I used only my feelings to reach a specific heart rate. [...] I just used the application to be sure." while another inexperienced one said "The Application. Using my feelings wouldn't work since I have no idea about my heart rate when

I am running.". Only one participant said he had big problems learning and remembering the heart rates in the learning phases. He also stated that he forgot
about the vibration while running.

Did the Application Distract You? Four participants said they were not
distracted by the application at all. One even stated that he liked the permanent
representation instead of looking at a heart rate monitor screen. Three participants felt very distracted, because they had to concentrate on the application.
They were not sure if that would be the same outside a study environment.
Others were distracted because they had to hold the device in their hand all
the time but not by the vibrations themselves. One participant mentioned that
using the device in combination with music may be difficult because you hear
and feel different rhythms.

Did the Application Disturb Your Walking/Running Rhythm? Four
participants did not feel disturbed by the vibration of the application. One felt
disturbed all the time. The other ones mentioned exactly one phase in which
their heart rate and their running rhythm interfered, so they were not able to
walk normally because they wanted to walk in the same speed as their heart
beat.

Additional Feedback Most of the participants did not like to hold a smart
phone in their hands all the time. One suggested to use a vibrating ball instead
which is easier to hold. Another one suggested to integrate the vibration into the
chest belt of the heart rate sensor. The idea itself to display the heart rate with
vibration was well accepted and described as comfortable. The vibration itself
was not felt in the same way by all participants. Sometimes it was mentioned
that the vibration was easy to feel ("It's surprising how good you can feel it
when running.") but also that it was hard to feel ("The vibration should be
stronger. It's hard to feel while running."). One participant even put the device
on his ear and said "it's easier to hear than to feel". It was also suggested not
to communicate every heartbeat but just every second one, because at higher
heart rates the vibrations are too frequent. In addition it was recommended that
the device be easy to switch on and off. Some participants thought that using
the device for a longer period of time would result in a good feeling for the
displayed frequency and therefore for the own heart rate. It was seen positively
that the application gives permanent feedback about the activity level. Generally,
the application was well accepted and commented as "cool", "exciting", and
"interesting". Some participants missed features of regular heart rate displays
like warnings at certain heart rates, but liked the permanent feedback.

4.4   Discussion

The interviews have shown that our participants generally like the idea of a
tactile heart rate display. They were often able to tell when their heart rate

deviated from the learned one by more than 10 bpm. The high deviation at 80 bpm for some participants is not surprising, because some reported that they were hardly able to reach such a low heart rate during the study or just did not want to wait until their heart rate dropped so low. In all cases but one the measured heart rate was a bit higher than the learned one. Most participants had a lower heart rate when they ended the learning part, so they may have wanted to raise it faster and started to walk or run faster than necessary. If such a tendency can be confirmed in future evaluations, a correction factor to the tactile pulse could be applied so the users would more likely reach the desired heart rate.

It is remarkable that all participants stated that the haptic pulse strengthened the awareness of their heart rate. This is very interesting when thinking about special needs of certain user groups. People with a heart disease, for example, may use such a haptic pulse device to learn more about their heart, not just during physical exercises, but also in their everyday live. Some participants even learned something about the behaviour of their heart during our short study, so a bigger learning effect may appear when using a haptic pulse device for a longer time period. To address the need for a warning at certain heart rates, some methods to simultaneously display the heart rate and these warnings have to be evaluated. Due to the fact that some participants felt disturbed at specific pulse rates it may be useful to make the device easy to turn off when it is used for a short time, like a heart rate watch.

A vibrating smart phone held in the hands seems to be in no way sufficient, especially when the device should be used over a longer period of time. The device is too loud in silent environments and the vibration is too weak when the device is not held in the hands during exercises. A device which can be safely attached to a sensitive part of the body and generates vibration impulses more or less intense with respect to the activity of the wearers may help to improve their experience.

5   Conclusions and Future Work

In this paper we evaluated a tactile representation of the heart rate during physical activities. In a user study with ten participants we collected qualitative feedback which can be used to built improved devices and enable a good user experience when a permanent heart rate display is needed or useful. Since many participants were also interested in a long term usage of the device, future research and development of wearable sensors and actors was encouraged. Because of the great improvement of the awareness of the heart rate, tests with people who actually need to learn about the behaviour of their heart rate like patients with a heart disease would be interesting. Regarding this learning effect it is also interesting whether the device can be removed and after what time span this is possible without loosing the benefits. The device could for example reduce the feedback over time, so that at first it displays the heart rate all the time and later only in certain situations or on demand of the user. Incorporating the technique into other health related applications, where the pure display and recording of the heart rate is not enough, may be useful. So they can benefit from the possible lower distraction and the learning effect. After all, we see a great potential in displaying the heart rate in a tactile way. In the future this concept may also be applied to other vital parameters like the breathing frequency to raise the awareness for reactions of the body to certain situations.

References

1. Achten, J., Jeukendrup, A.E.: Heart rate monitoring. Sports Med. 33(7), 517–538 (2003)
2. Albinet, C., Boucard, G., Bouquet, C., Audiffren, M.: Increased heart rate variability and executive performance after aerobic training in the elderly. European Journal of Applied Physiology 109(4), 617–624 (2010)
3. Asif, A., Boll, S.: Where to turn my car?: comparison of a tactile display and a conventional car navigation system under high load condition. In: Proceedings of the 2nd International Conference on Automotive User Interfaces and Interactive Vehicular Applications, pp. 64–71. ACM (2010)
4. Brewster, S., Brown, L.: Tactons: structured tactile messages for non-visual information display. In: Proceedings of the Fifth Conference on Australasian User Interface, vol. 28, pp. 15–23. Australian Computer Society, Inc. (2004)
5. Gamelin, F.X., Berthoin, S., Sayah, H., Libersa, C., Bosquet, L.: Effect of training and detraining on heart rate variability in healthy young men. International Journal of Sports Medicine 28(7), 564–570 (2007)
6. Lotan, G., Croft, C.: Impulse. In: CHI 2007 Extended Abstracts on Human Factors in Computing Systems, pp. 1983–1988. ACM (2007)
7. Pielot, M., Krull, O., Boll, S.: Where is my team: supporting situation awareness with tactile displays. In: Proceedings of the 28th International Conference on Human Factors in Computing Systems, pp. 1705–1714. ACM (2010)
8. Thayer, J., Åhs, F., Fredrikson, M., Sollers III, J., Wager, T.: A meta-analysis of heart rate variability and neuroimaging studies: Implications for heart rate variability as a marker of stress and health. Neuroscience & Biobehavioral Reviews (2011)
9. Werner, J., Wettach, R., Hornecker, E.: United-pulse: feeling your partner's pulse. In: Proceedings of the 10th International Conference on Human Computer Interaction with Mobile Devices and Services, pp. 535–538. ACM (2008)
10. Wisløff, U., Støylen, A., Loennechen, J., Bruvold, M., Rognmo, Ø., Haram, P., Tjønna, A., Helgerud, J., Slørdahl, S., Lee, S., et al.: Superior cardiovascular effect of aerobic interval training versus moderate continuous training in heart failure patients. Circulation 115(24), 3086–3094 (2007)

Audio-Haptic Simulation of Walking on Virtual Ground Surfaces to Enhance Realism

Niels C. Nilsson, Rolf Nordahl, Luca Turchet, and Stefania Serafin

Medialogy, Department of Architecture, Design and Media Technology
Aalborg University Copenhagen
{ncn,rn,sts,tur}@create.aau.dk

Abstract. In this paper we describe two experiments whose goal is to investigate the role of physics-based auditory and haptic feedback provided at feet level to enhance realism in a virtual environment. To achieve this goal, we designed a multimodal virtual environment where subjects could walk on a platform overlooking a canyon. Subjects were asked to visit the environment wearing an head-mounted display and a custom made pair of sandals enhanced with sensors and actuators. A 12-channels surround sound system delivered a soundscape which was consistent with the visual environment. In the first experiment, passive haptics was provided by having a physical wooden platform present in the laboratory. In the second experiment, no passive haptics was present. In both experiments, subjects reported of having a more realistic experience while auditory and haptic feedback are present. However, measured physiological data and post-experimental presence questionnaire do not show significant differences when audio-haptic feedback is provided.

1 Introduction

When navigating in a physical place by walking, several nonvisual cues are provided, such as the feel of the surface a person is stumpling upon, the sound of footsteps and the soundscape of the environment. In order to create realistic simulations of walking in a virtual place, it is desirable to reproduce such cues in a virtual environment.

In this paper, we are interested in investigating one's awareness of auditory and haptic feedback in foot based devices, topic which is still rather unexplored in the virtual reality community. Virtual augmented footwear has interesting applications in different fields related to virtual reality. As an example, auditory and haptic feedback in foot-based interaction can assist rehabilitation. Moreover, feet-based interfaces has started to appear in the entertainment industry, in the form of platforms such as the Wii fit from Nintendo, which is connected to the Wii console.[1] Having the possibility to provide auditory and haptic feedback has the potential of providing interesting applications in the field of navigation, especially for visually impaired people, rehabilitation and entertainment.

---

[1] www.nintendo.com

C. Magnusson, D. Szymczak, and S. Brewster (Eds.): HAID 2012, LNCS 7468, pp. 61–70, 2012.
© Springer-Verlag Berlin Heidelberg 2012

2   Previous Work

In the academic community, foot-based interactions have mostly been concerned with the engineering of locomotion interfaces for virtual environments [8]. A notable exception is the work of Paradiso and coworkers, who pioneered the development of shoes enhanced with sensors, able to capture 16 different parameters such as pressure, orientation, acceleration [7]. Such shoes were used for entertainment purpose as well as for rehabilitation studies [1]. The company Nike has also developed an accelerometer which can be attached to running shoes and connected to an iPod, in such a way that, when a person runs, the iPod tracks and reports different information. Shoes enhanced with sensors and actuators were presented in [6], and an experiment was run in order to evaluate ability of subjects to recognize the virtual simulated surfaces driven by such shoes. Results showed that subjects were able to recognize simulated surfaces when rendered both using auditory and haptic at feet level.

However, to our knowledge the use of footwear augmented with sensors and actuators has not been investigated yet when combined with visual feedback in a virtual reality experience. While active haptic feedback at feet level has not been investigated yet in a virtual reality environment, passive haptics is known to significantly enhance presence [3]. Passive haptics has also been combined with redirected walking in [4].

In this paper, we are interested in investigating whether realism in a virtual reality environment is increased by enhancing the simulation with interactive auditory and haptic feedback provided at the feet. To achieve this goal, we engineered a pair of shoes enhanced with sensors and actuators. While wearing the shoes, subjects are able to hear and feel the surfaces they are stumpling upon. Our hypothesis is that this enhanced simulation has an impact on the perceived realism of the simulation and also sense of presence reported by the subjects in the environment.

To validate our hypotheses, as done in [5], we measured both physiological data while the subjects performed the experiments, and we also asked subjects to fill a post-experimental presence questionnaire. Measuring physiological data is essentially based on the assumption that a user, experiencing an intense sense of presence in a virtual environment, will exhibit physiological and behavioral responses comparable to those produced while experiencing a similar real world environment [9].

Moreover, after completing the experiment we asked subjects whether they were able to notice any difference among the experimental conditions they were exposed to.

We start by briefly describing the technology developed, and we then present two experiments whose goal is to evaluate the ability of auditory and haptic feedback to enhance realism and presence in the simulated virtual environment.

3   A Multimodal Architecture

We have developed a multimodal architecture with the goal of creating audio-haptic-visual simulations of walking-based interactions. The system requires users to walk around a space wearing a pair of shoes enhanced with sensors and actuators.

The architecture consists of a pair of custom made shoes enhanced with sensors and actuators. On top of the shoes, markers are place to track the position of the feet by using an Optitrack motion capture system by Naturalpoint. Auditory feedback is provided using a surround sound system composed by 12 Dynaudio BM5A speakers, and visual feedback is provided by a nVisor SX head-mounted display (HMD), with 1280x1024 resolution in each eye and a diagonal FOV of 60 degrees.

In order to provide auditory and haptic feedback during the act of walking, a pair of custom made shoes with sensors and actuators has been recently developed. The technology is described in [11].

4   Simulation Software

We developed a multimodal physics-based synthesis engine able to reproduce auditory and haptic feedback at feet level, to simulate the act of walking on different surfaces. An interesting characteristic of this engine is its ability to physically simulate both auditory and haptic feedback. The footstep synthesis engine, is able to render the sounds of footsteps both on solid and aggregate surfaces. Several different materials have been simulated, in particular wood, creaking wood, and metal as concerns the solid surfaces, and gravel, snow, sand, dirt, forest underbrush, dry leaves, and high grass as regards the aggregate surfaces. A complete description of such engine in terms of sound design, implementation and control systems is presented in [12].

In this particular experiment, the engine was tuned in order to simulate the audio and haptic sensation of walking on a creaking wooden plank. This particular material was chosen to match the visual feedback provided to the subjects. The synthesis engine works in realtime and is driven by the shoes described in the previous section.

4.1   Visual Feedback

The goal of the visual feedback is to render, through the use of a commercial game engine, the visual sensation of exploring a canyon. In particular, in our simulation the Unity3D game engine has been used (http://unity3d.com/). This engine was used for its ability to render realistic visual environments without being skilled visual designers. This choice was ideal for us, since our main interest is a physically based audio-haptic engine, so the visual feedback is used only for supporting it, without being the main goal. Figure 1 shows one view of the visual feedback provided to the users and one user performing the experiment. As can be seen in the left side of Figure 1, subjects are able to see a representation of their own feet when looking down in the virtual environment. This feature was implemented since it has been demonstrated that when using an HMD presence is enhanced when visual body feedback is provided [2].

5   Experiment Design

We designed two experiments whose goal was to investigate the role of auditory and haptic feedback in enhancing presence and realism in the simulated virtual environment. As can be seen in Figure 1, in the first experiment subjects were asked to stand on a physical wooden plank while experiencing the environment. Such plank was not present in the second experiment. The reason was to investigate whether passive haptic had an effect in the results.

Fig. 1. One participant performing the test (left) and a view of the environment (right)

Both experiments were designed as within-subjects experiments, where half of the subjects experienced the condition without audio-haptic feedback (named NF in the following) first and the one with audio-haptic feedback (named F in the following) afterwards, while the other half experienced the condition with audio-haptic feedback first and the one without audio-haptic feedback afterwards.

5.1   Equipment and Task

Before starting the experiment, each participant was asked to wear the HMD and haptic shoes previously described, together with a wireless Q sensor device developed by Affectiva (www.affectiva.com), which, placed around the wrist, allows to measure skin conductance and temperature. Subjects were instructed that their task was to find three objects in the environment: a backpack, a camera and a hat. Subjects were also asked to wear a wireless device able to measure heart beat (Scosche mytrek wireless pulse monitor). After being ready to start the experiment, subjects were taken on the wooden platform, for those subjects exposed to the condition with passive feedback. For about a minute, subjects were allowed to freely explore the visual environment. In addition to allowing the participants to become familiar with the equipment, the hope was that this would minimize the effects of the orienting effect, that is, individuals usually elicit a stronger physiological response the first time they are exposed to a given stimulus event [5].

The objects were sufficiently hard to see in such a way to encourage subjects to explore the environment. After two minutes, subjects were asked to stop their search and to complete a presence questionnaire described later. Once subjects were done with the questionnaire, they were asked to repeat the experiment with the other condition. After two minutes, subjects were again asked to stop the experience of visiting the environment and asked to fill the same presence questionnaire. At the end of the experiment, subjects were asked questions to assess their ability of recognizing the feedback provided.

5.2 Participants

Forty participants were divided in two groups (n=20) to perform the two experiments. The two groups were composed respectively of 15 men and 5 women, aged between 20 and 34 (mean=23.05, standard deviation=3.13), and of 15 men and 5 women, aged between 20 and 32 (mean=23.5, standard deviation=3.17). Participants were primarily recruited from the campus of the Media Technology Department of the Aalborg University Copenhagen; however no restrictions on background were imposed. All participants reported normal, or corrected to normal, hearing. Participants were primarily recruited from the campus of the Media Technology Department of the Aalborg University Copenhagen; however no restrictions on background were imposed.

Participants were not awarded after the completion of the study. They were provided an informed consent form discussing the possible effects of participation in the study. Additionally, participants were informed that they could stop at any time during the experiment.

6 Results

In this section we present the results of both experiments, discussing the importance of feedback by examining both the case with passive haptics and the case without passive haptics.

6.1 Physiological Measures of Presence

Table 1 and Table 2 show the results pertaining to the measures of skin conductance and skin temperature.

The skin temperature and skin conductance measures used during the experiment including passive haptic feedback did generally not suggest an increase in presence as a consequence of the added feedback. It is possible that the skin temperature measure have been corrupted by the orienting effect, individuals usually elicit a stronger physiological response the first time they are exposed to a given stimulus event. The results suggest that the participants in average experienced an increase in skin temperature between the first and the second trial, regardless of what condition was experienced first.

Table 1. Mean and standard deviation skin temperature (degrees celsius) for the two condition-orders NF-F and F-NF

	NF-F		F-NF	
Condition	NF	F	NF	F
With PH	29.46 ± 0.80	30.27 ± 1.09	30,51 ± 0,95	29,92 ± 0,79
Without PH	31.19 ± 0.63	30.71 ± 0.62	30.42 ± 0.70	31.01 ± 0.69

Table 2. Mean skin conductance (microSiemens) for the two condition-orders NF-F and F-NF

	NF-F		F-NF	
Condition	NF	F	NF	F
With PH	1,69 ± 2,15	1,71 ± 1,68	1,54 ± 1,87	1,29 ± 1,37
Without PH	5.79 ± 8.18	4.80 ± 8.41	2.07 ± 2.43	2.30 ± 2.35

Note that these differences were statistically significant ($p(19) = -5,4930$, $p \leq 0.05$). Similarly, significant difference was found between the averages pertaining to the skin temperature in case of both condition orders (NF-F: $t(9) = 7945$, $p = \leq 0.05$ and F-NF: $t(9) = -4.1416$, $p \leq 0.05$). It is possible to offer at least two explanations for this set of results, one being that the participants generally found the first exposure to the VE the scariest and therefore had a lower skin temperature during the first trial. A second explanation is that the high temperature within the laboratory caused their temperature to rise gradually for the duration of the experiment. Notably, the one explanation does not preclude the other. The results obtained from the skin conductance measure are inconclusive at best since no meaningful tendencies are present. The measures of skin temperature and skin conductance applied during the experiment where passive haptic feedback yielded similar results. It is worth noting that there is a significant difference between the averages pertaining to the skin temperature in case of both condition orders for the experiment without passive haptic feedback. (NF-F: $t(9) = 4.6577$, $p = \leq 0.05$ and F-NF: $t(9) = -5,0466$, $p \leq 0.05$). As was the case with the experiment including passive haptic feedback, it seems possible that the participants have experienced less stress or fear during the second condition or simply have gotten gradually warmer due to the high temperature in the lab. Moreover, there was a significant difference between the mean skin conductance during condition order NF-F ($t(9) = 2,5008$, $p \leq 0.05$). However, the corresponding means related to condition order F-NF did not differ significantly. With this being said, it should be stressed that a significant difference would not have changed the fact that these results do not suggest that the participants experienced a higher level of presence during the condition with added feedback. Regardless of the condition order the participants seem to have experienced an increase in skin conduction from the first to the second condition, which suggests a higher degree of skin perspiration. Notably a comparison by means of paired sample t-test revealed that there is a significant difference between the first and second trial, both in case of skin temperature ($p(19) = -6,946$, $p \leq 0.05$) and skin conductance ($p(19) = -2,4511$, ≤ 0.05).

Table 3 shows the results for the heart-rate measurements in the two experiments. As it is possible to notice, the average values in both the conditions and in both the experiments are always higher for the typology of stimuli presented first. In particular the statistical analysis conducted by means of a paired t-test revealed that such differences are significant for the heart-rate mean and maximum of the condition F-NF in the first experiment ($t(9) = 4.7555$, $p \leq 0.5$ and $t(9) = 3.0251$, $p \leq 0.5$ respectively), and for the heart-rate mean and maximum of the condition NF-F in the second experiment ($t(9) = 3.4804$, $p \leq 0.5$ and $t(9) = 5.0558$, $p \leq 0.5$ respectively).

Note there is a significant difference between the averages pertaining to the skin temperature in case of both condition orders. This can be interpreted in two different, albeit

Table 3. Heart-rate results of the experiment with passive haptics. Legenda: NF-F: trials in which the no feedback condition was presented first and the feedback condition afterwards; F-NF: trials in which the feedback condition was presented first and the no feedback condition afterwards.

WITH PH	Trials NF-F			Trials F-NF		
	Mean	Max.	Min.	Mean	Max.	Min.
NF	90±13.96	99.2±14.92	81.9±14.45	89.2±15	97.2±14.28	83.7±15.83
F	87.5±11.17	96.9±8.68	78.6±11.89	93.3±14.17	101.6±14.71	86.2±15.12
WITHOUT PH	Mean	Max.	Min.	Mean	Max.	Min.
NF	92.2±9.54	103.3±10.97	84.1±9.38	86.1±10.21	95.8±11.79	77.6±8.07
F	88.1±8.19	94.4±10.04	82.2±9.24	89.6±14.45	99.3±19.04	79.5±10.69

not necessary mutually exclusive, ways. First, the participants may have experienced less stress or fear during the second condition. Secondly, it is possible that the participants got gradually warmer as due to the hight temperature in the lab. Moreover, there was a significant difference between the mean skin conductance during condition order NF-F. The corresponding means related to condition order F-NF were not significantly different ($p = 0.2$).

6.2 Self-reported Measures of Presence

The participants experience of presence was assessed by means of the Slater-Usoh-Steed (SUS) questionnaire [10], [13], which is a questionnaire intended to evaluate the experience after exposures to a virtual environment (VE). The SUS questionnaire contains six items that evaluate the experience of presence in terms of, the participants sense of being in the VE, the extent to which the participant experienced the VE as the dominant reality, and the extent to which the VE is remembered as a place. All items are answered on scales ranging from 1 to 7 where the highest scores would be indicative of presence [13]:

Q1: Please rate your sense of being in the virtual environment, on a scale of 1 to 7, where 7 represents your normal experience of being in a place.
Q2: To what extent were there times during the experience when the virtual environment was the reality for you?
Q3: When you think back to the experience, do you think of the virtual environment more as images that you saw or more as somewhere that you visited?
Q4: During the time of the experience, which was the strongest on the whole, your sense of being in the virtual environment or of being elsewhere?
Q5: Consider your memory of being in the virtual environment. How similar in terms of the structure of the memory is this to the structure of the memory of other places you have been today?
Q6: During the time of your experience, did you often think to yourself that you were actually in the virtual environment?

The general level of presence experienced by the participants may be determined by summarizing the data obtained from the all of the questionnaire items in two ways.

First, one may present the central tendency as the mean of all ratings to all items and the variability may thus be presented as the corresponding standard deviation. Secondly, it is possible to present the general experience of presence across participants (SUS count), as the mean of the individual presence scores. The presence score is taken as the sum of scores of 6 and 7 out of the number of questions posed [13].

Tables 4 illustrates the questionnaire's evaluations for the two experiments.

Table 4. Questionnaire results of both experiments

	Trials NF-F		Trials F-NF	
WITH PH	NF	F	NF	F
Q1	5.3±1.49	6±1.15	5.63±1.2	5.45±1.12
Q2	5.5±1.08	5.6±1.26	5.45±1.36	5.45±1.12
Q3	3.9±1.79	5.1±1.59	5.09±1.57	5.81±0.98
Q4	5.9±0.99	6.1±0.56	5.18±1.53	6.18±0.87
Q5	3.5±1.5	4.7±1.63	4.72±1.79	4.54±0.93
Q6	4.9±1.72	5.3±1.7	5.09±2.02	6.18±1.16
SUS count	0.38±2.13	0.65±2.16	0.6±0.89	0.6±2.52
WITHOUT PH	NF	F	NF	F
Q1	4.7±1.15	5.4±1.26	5.3±1.56	5.6±0.96
Q2	4.±1.15	5.±1.33	4.8±1.22	5.3±0.94
Q3	4.5±1.77	4.7±1.56	4.8±1.68	4.8±1.68
Q4	5.4±1.07	5.3±1.15	5.5±0.97	5.3±1.15
Q5	3.9±2.55	4.3±2.49	4.1±1.79	4.2±2.14
Q6	3.6±1.57	5.2±1.68	5.7±1.25	4.9±1.37
SUS count	0.28±1.17	0.5±1.41	0.46±1.75	0.41±0.75

As outlined in [13], to check if the differences found in the questionnaire results for the two typologies of stimuli F and NF are statistically significant, one should not compare the means of the questionnaire items results, but rather the number of answers having a score of 6 or 7. Following this approach we found statistical significance in both the experiments (with and without passive haptics) for the trials in which the no feedback condition was presented first and the feedback condition afterwards ($\chi^2(1) = 5.0364$, p-value = 0.02482 and $\chi^2(1) = 7.5083$, p-value = 0.006141 respectively). Conversely, no significance was found in none of the two experiments for the trials in which the feedback condition was presented first and the no feedback condition afterwards. While the choice of the SUS-presence questionnaire was motivated by the fact that it is extensively validated and used in the VR community, it can be questioned whether it is the most suitable for examining the relationship between feedback and presence.

6.3   Realism and Audio-Haptic Feedback

As a final analysis of the experiments' results, it is interesting to discuss the observations provided by the subjects when the experiments were completed. Specifically, we asked subjects if they had noticed any difference on the two conditions and, in affirmative case, if they could elaborate on the differences noticed and how they affected their experience.

During the first experiment, when asked whether they had noticed a difference between the two trials, 13 of the participants mentioned that they had noticed the change in the haptic and/or auditory feedback provided by the shoes. Precisely, 5 subjects noticed a difference in both auditory and haptic feedback, 7 only noticed the difference in auditory feedback, while 1 only noticed the difference in haptic feedback. All of the participants who noticed the difference expressed a preference towards the added feedback. When asked to elaborate, 11 of the 13 stated that it added realism, 5 felt that it made the experience more scary or intensified the sensation of vertigo, while 1 explicitly stated that it increased the sensation of presence in the virtual environment.

During the second experiment, out of the 20 participants, 16 noticed the additional feedback, 5 participants noticed both the auditory and haptic feedback while 7 just noticed the sound and 4 only noticed the haptic feedback. With one exception, all of the participants who noticed the difference preferred the additional feedback. The one participant who did not, described that he did like the haptic feedback, but he had found it too intense. Out of the 16 who noticed the feedback 13 thought that it added realism, 2 described that it made it more scary and 2 explicitly stated that it intensified the sensation of being there.

Such observations show that subjects indeed were able to notice and appreciate the provided feedback in both experimentals' conditions. The lack of the same evidence while analyzing physiological data or presence questionnaire can be due to the fact that the provided feedback does not necessarily elicit a higher physiological response or sense of presence.

7   Conclusion and Future Work

In this paper, we have described two experiments whose goal was to assess the role of auditory and haptic feedback delivered at feet level to enhance sense of presence and realism in a multimodal virtual environments. The first experiment was performed with passive haptics, while subjects were experiencing the environment with and without auditory and haptic feedback. The second experiment was performed without passive haptics. While quantitative results obtained while measuring physiological data and performing a post-experimental presence questionnaire do not show significant differences among the two conditions, subjects were actually able to perceive the differences among the experiences. As discussed in the paper, indeed several subjects noticed the auditory and haptic feedback and reported on appreciating it and experiencing it as a way to simulate realism and sense of "being there".

In the future, we are interested in further investigating the role of auditory and haptic feedback provided at feet-level, also as a mean to provide useful information such as indications for navigation in virtual environments or feedback for actions in computer games.

References

1. Benbasat, A., Morris, S., Paradiso, J.: A wireless modular sensor architecture and its application in on-shoe gait analysis. In: Proceedings of IEEE Sensors 2003, vol. 2 (2003)
2. Bruder, G., Steinicke, F., Rothaus, K., Hinrichs, K.: Enhancing presence in head-mounted display environments by visual body feedback using head-mounted cameras. In: 2009 International Conference on CyberWorlds, pp. 43–50. IEEE (2009)
3. Insko, B.: Passive haptics significantly enhances virtual environments. PhD thesis, Citeseer (2001)
4. Kohli, L., Burns, E., Miller, D., Fuchs, H.: Combining passive haptics with redirected walking. In: Proceedings of the 2005 International Conference on Augmented Tele-Existence, pp. 253–254. ACM (2005)
5. Meehan, M., Insko, B., Whitton, M., Brooks Jr., F.: Physiological measures of presence in stressful virtual environments. ACM Transactions on Graphics (TOG) 21, 645–652 (2002)
6. Nordahl, R., Berrezag, A., Dimitrov, S., Turchet, L., Hayward, V., Serafin, S.: Preliminary experiment combining virtual reality haptic shoes and audio synthesis. Haptics: Generating and Perceiving Tangible Sensations, 123–129 (2010)
7. Paradiso, J., Hsiao, K., Hu, E.: Interactive music for instrumented dancing shoes. In: Proc. of the 1999 International Computer Music Conference, pp. 453–456 (1999)
8. Pelah, A., Koenderink, J.J.: Editorial: Walking in real and virtual environments. ACM Transactions on Applied Perception (TAP) 4(1), 1 (2007)
9. Slater, M., Lotto, B., Arnold, M.M., Sanchez-Vives, M.V.: How we experience immersive virtual environments: the concept of presence and its measurement. Anuario de Psicologia 40(2), 193–210 (2009)
10. Slater, M., Usoh, M., Steed, A.: Depth of presence in immersive virtual environments. Presence: Teleoperators and Virtual Environments 3(2), 130–144 (1994)
11. Turchet, L., Nordahl, R., Berrezag, A., Dimitrov, S., Hayward, V., Serafin, S.: Audio-haptic physically based simulation of walking on different grounds. In: Proceedings of IEEE International Workshop on Multimedia Signal Processing, pp. 269–273. IEEE Press (2010)
12. Turchet, L., Serafin, S., Dimitrov, S., Nordahl, R.: Physically based sound synthesis and control of footsteps sounds. In: Proceedings of Digital Audio Effects Conference, pp. 161–168 (2010)
13. Usoh, M., Catena, E., Arman, S., Slater, M.: Using presence questionnaires in reality. Presence: Teleoperators and Virtual Environments 9(5), 497–503 (2000)

Interacting with Deformable User Interfaces: Effect of Material Stiffness and Type of Deformation Gesture

Johan Kildal

Nokia Research Center, Helsinki, Finland
johan.kildal@nokia.com

Abstract. Deformable User Interfaces (DUIs) are increasingly being proposed for new tangible and organic interaction metaphors and techniques. To design DUIs, it is necessary to understand how deforming different materials manually using different gestures affects performance and user experience. In the study reported in this paper, three DUIs made of deformable materials with different levels of stiffness were used in navigation tasks that required bending and twisting the interfaces. Discrete and continuous deformation gestures were used in each case. Results showed that the stiffness of the material and the type of gesture affected performance and user experience in complex ways, but with a pervading pattern: using discrete gestures in very short navigation distances and continuous gestures otherwise, plus using lower-stiffness materials in every case, was beneficial in terms of performance and user experience.

Keywords: deformable, organic, tangible, user interface, force, bend, twist, zoom, scroll, stiffness, gesture, discrete, continuous, performance, UX.

1 Introduction

Deformable User Interfaces (DUIs) lie in the intersection between Organic User Interfaces (OUIs) [1] and Tangible User Interfaces (TUIs) [2]. They consist of physical objects that are intended to be grasped and manipulated with the hands in order to interact with a system. The manipulation of a DUI results in the physical deformation of the material the object is made of. Thus, deforming the interface elastically or plastically is the distinctive form of input to the system when using a DUI. Such deformations are designed to give physical form to the interaction with information.

Functional deformable prototypes that implement deformation interactions as they have been envisioned are still difficult to build. Examples include crumpling and restoring a display [3], and new device concepts that are heavily based on new nanotechnological sensors and materials [4, 5]. Meanwhile, HCI is advancing based on *ad-hoc* DUI prototypes with targeted functionality [6-10], or non-functional prototypes used in qualitative studies [3]. DUIs can come in very different sizes and shapes. In the literature, we find that paper-inspired DUIs [3, 6-8] have received most of the attention. Examples of alternative approaches include the manipulation of raw material [9, 10]. In all of them, a common integral part of the interaction is that the user exerts forces on the interface, causing deformation of the material.

C. Magnusson, D. Szymczak, and S. Brewster (Eds.): HAID 2012, LNCS 7468, pp. 71–80, 2012.
© Springer-Verlag Berlin Heidelberg 2012

Many such deformation gestures have been proposed in earlier work. However, the impact that the physical characteristics of different deformable materials have on the execution of these gestures has not been studied systematically. Only Lee *et al.* [3] compared deformation gestures with interfaces made of different materials, but their prototypes were non-functional and the interactions imaginary. To address this gap, in this paper we report a study that takes a first look at the stiffness of a deformable material as a design parameter. In particular, we investigate how material stiffness affects performance and user experience when performing whole-device deformations in navigation tasks (twisting to scroll and bending to zoom), using either discrete or continuous gestures. Three functional DUIs were used, which were identical in their smartphone-like form factor but different in the stiffness of the material they were made of. With this study, we address part of the research agenda proposed in [11].

2   Research Study

2.1   Deformable Hardware

We built a family of functional DUI research prototypes (called *Kinetic DUI-RP*) [11], which could be bent and twisted using both hands. Each prototype consisted of two rigid parts joined by a 62mm-long central body made of deformable material. The rigid parts afforded holding the device and exerting torque actions. Each research prototype (RP) contained a set of deformation sensors (strain gauges) that could detect bending and twisting of the deformable body with 10-bit accuracy and 200Hz sample rates. In this study, three Kinetic DUI-RP interfaces were employed, which were built using different deformable materials in the central section. The deformable material in each prototype presented a different rotational stiffness, and consequently different amount of force was required from a user to bend and twist each prototype. The three prototypes could detect bend and twist deformations of up to 25 degrees away from the resting flat position (Fig. 1). As the Kinetic DUI-RPs did not include a visual display, they were connected to an external computer display.

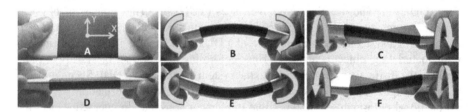

Fig. 1. Main axes of a Kinetic DUI-RP (A). Bend up gesture (B). Twist down gesture (C). Resting position (D). Bend down gesture (E). Twist up gesture (F).

2.2   Experimental Design

An experiment was designed in which navigation through schematic information spaces was performed by bending or twisting the prototypes. Two independent variables (IVs) were selected: stiffness of deformable body and type of gesture.

Navigation Task. We devised a one-dimensional navigation task for each deformation gesture: zooming for bending, and list-scrolling for twisting. These tasks were chosen for being intuitive according to taxonomies [3, 8] and to our own pilot research. From an interaction perspective, both tasks were implemented to be equivalent in every other respect. The GUIs showed schematic representations of the information spaces, as shown in Fig. 2. In both cases, the space was divided into 12 zones (concentric rectangles for zooming, and stacked horizontal slots for scrolling). The position of a red cursor (a thin rectangle or a horizontal line) was controlled by the user. When the cursor entered the area of the target, this was highlighted with the target zone changing its color. If the cursor remained within the target continuously for 2 seconds (*dwell* selection), the task was complete.

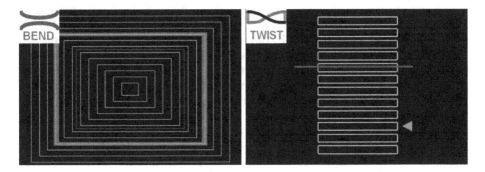

Fig. 2. GUI representations for bend-to-zoom (left) and twist-to-scroll (right)

Stiffness of the Deformable Material. The three levels of stiffness selected (measured as rotational stiffness, in *N·m/rad*), were: 2.5 (highest stiffness), 1.3 (medium stiffness), and 0.45 (lowest stiffness). All three values are well below the threshold of perception of rigidity [12], meaning that even the most rigid of these interfaces felt clearly deformable when manipulated. In addition, the differences between them were well above JNDs [13], thus being clearly discriminable from each other when manipulated.

Type of Deformation Gesture. Two types of deformation gestures were compared: *continuous* and *discrete*. When using continuous gestures, bending or twisting the device beyond a threshold angle (4.5 degrees) started to displace the cursor. In bend-to-zoom, the rectangular cursor changed in size: bend up/down to zoom in/out (Fig. 1, B and E). Similarly, in twist-to-scroll the cursor line displaced vertically: twist up/down to scroll up/down (Fig. 1, F and C). The speed of displacement of the cursor was proportional to the amount that the interface was deformed beyond the threshold. A broad range of speeds could be attained in this way, between 0.02 and 8.6 zones/s.

Discrete gestures, on the contrary, were performed in a "deform-and-restore" fashion. The GUI representation and the direction of the mappings were the same. However, every time a discrete gesture was performed, the cursor displaced instantaneously by one full position. The action was triggered when the deformation surpassed a threshold angle of 10 degrees. To trigger another step, the interface had to be restored to its resting position and then deformed again. Thus, the speed of the navigation depended on the frequency at which deform-and-restore cycles were performed.

Experimental Procedure. A 2-way (2x3) repeated-measures experiment was designed. The IVs were the *rotational stiffness* of the device (*High, Medium* and *Low*), and the *type of deformation gesture* (*Discrete* and *Continuous*). In each of the six conditions, 40 repetitions of a navigation task were presented in random order, 20 repetitions requiring the use of bend to zoom, and the other 20 using twist to scroll. Of the 20 repetitions of each navigation task, half (10) started with the cursor located at each end of the navigation space (at the outermost/innermost rectangle for zooming, or at the topmost/bottommost slot for scrolling). The target could be located at 10 different distances, between 1 and 10 positions away. Thus, the target was never located at the very end of the navigation space. This was done to preserve the possibility of overshooting the target in every repetition As a result, the strategy of navigating at maximum speed to the other end was impractical. A label and a graphic representation of that gesture were displayed on the top-left corner of the GUI. This eased the mental demand of identifying the gesture to be used in each new task (Fig. 2).

Twelve participants were recruited for this study: 8 male (1 left handed); 4 female (2 left-handed); aged 27-42 (M=35; SD= 5.5). The order of presentation of the conditions was counterbalanced as follows: six participants completed the three conditions with continuous gestures first, and then the three conditions with discrete gestures (counterbalancing the order in each case). The other six participants completed the conditions in the inverse order. No time limit was imposed for the completion of each task. Each condition was followed by filling in a standard NASA-TLX questionnaire [14] with an additional *preference* category. Each session ended with a brief semi-structured interview to further assess the UX.

3   Results

3.1   Performance

The normalized time (NT) to reach the target (i.e. the time per unit of distance to the target) was selected as a measure of the performance across different conditions. The total time used to calculate NT started to be counted when the threshold of displacement was first surpassed, i.e. when the cursor started to displace for the first time. The 2 seconds of dwell time at the end of the task were not included as part of the total time. Thus, the task was timed until the cursor entered the area of the target for the last time before a successful dwell selection.

A two-way repeated-measures ANOVA test was conducted to analyze NT. It was found that both the rotational stiffness of the device [$F(2,22)=12.53$, $p<0.001$] and the type of gesture [$F(1,11)=77.63$, $p\approx0$] had statistically significant effects on NT (Fig. 3), with no significant interactions between the IVs [$F(2,22)=0.43$, $p=0.66$].

Looking into each IV, NT increased significantly with the stiffest material (Fig. 3, left). Post-hoc analysis (Fischer's $LSD_{95\%}$[1] = 0.037) showed that the significant differences were observed between the material with high stiffness (M=0.365s; SD=0.11) and both the material with medium (M=0.323s; SD=0.118) and with low stiffness (M=0.301s; SD=0.104), with no significant difference between the last two. Regarding the type of gesture (Fig. 3, right), NT was significantly higher (less efficient) with continuous gestures (M=0.412s; SD=0.097) than with discrete gestures (M=0.253s; SD=0.055).

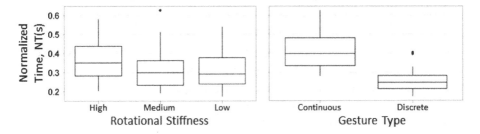

Fig. 3. Average normalized time, NT (time per unit of distance) for different levels of rotational stiffness (left) and gesture types (right)

Further analysis of the data regarding the effect of the gesture type revealed that this effect was more complex than just described. Fig. 4 shows NT graphically represented as a function of the initial distance to the target. Separate graphs are shown for bend-to-zoom and for twist-to-scroll tasks. In both cases, it can be observed that for short navigation distances discrete gestures were more efficient than continuous ones, and this is the dominant effect in the ANOVA (Fig. 3, right). However, for longer distances, continuous gestures became more efficient. Approximate cutting distances for the more efficient gesture type were found to be: 8 distance units for bending and 4 distance units for twisting (see crossing points for the Local Polynomial Regression Fitting – Loess – trend curves in Fig. 4).

Also in Fig. 4 it can be seen that, for discrete gestures, there was no apparent difference between bending and twisting for the behavior of TM over the distances to target. Instead, the difference in TM was most acute for continuous gestures and short navigation distances. In such cases, navigation by bending was far less efficient than navigating by twisting. These observations suggest that initiating, stopping and inverting input torques is done more easily when twisting the device than when bending it. Consequently, this difference becomes apparent in short distance navigations, where the initiation and termination of the navigation accounts for a bigger fraction of the complete navigation process. A hypothesis to explain this difference is that it may be easier to exert pairs of forces around some axes of the prototype than others. Holding the device with both hands as shown in Fig. 1 allowed twisting the interface up and down without changing the way it was held: the length of the thumb resting above and the fingers aligned below could easily redistribute forces to create pairs with enough arm distance in either direction around the X axis (Fig. 1, A), without having to

---

[1] Fischer's Least Significant Difference.

change the position of the thumb or the fingers. To bend the prototype, however, the same way of holding it offered no arm distance to produce pairs of forces around its Y axis in such an easy way. In fact, a tendency was observed to reposition the fingers to bend up (the thumbs moved apart towards the edge and the fingers pushed from below) or to bend down (the fingers moved towards the edge and the thumb pushed from above). In addition, bigger dispersion in the data was observed when using continuous gestures in bending tasks, suggesting that participants employed a larger variety of procedures to bend than to twist with continuous gestures. Further research will help understand better these interesting ergonomic aspects of the interaction.

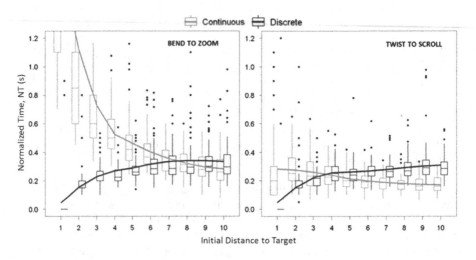

Fig. 4. NT as a function of the initial distance to the target. *Left:* bend-to-zoom. *Right* twist-to-scroll. Trends are shown by Local Polynomial Regression Fitting (Loess) curves.

3.2   Subjective Workload

NASA Task Load Index (TLX) [14] was used to assess quantitatively the relative subjective workload between conditions. For each condition, participants provided ratings on the 20-point scales of the six TLX questionnaire categories: *mental demand, physical demand, temporal demand, performance, effort,* and *frustration*. From these ratings, the overall subjective task load index (TLX) was calculated for each condition. Fig. 5 shows these results graphically. These results were analyzed calculating 2-way repeated-measures ANOVAs for the index and for each sub-category.

The outcome of this analysis is summarized in Table 1. The main finding regarding subjective workload was that none of the IVs had a statistically significant main effect on the overall TLX index. This analysis did, however, reveal some statistically significant main effects from both IVs on several of the sub-categories. It particular, the medium-stiffness prototype led to significantly lower levels of *mental demand*, as well as to higher levels of *performance* when compared to the other two prototypes. Regarding the effect of the type of gesture, discrete gestures led to significantly higher levels of *physical demand, time pressure* and *effort expended*.

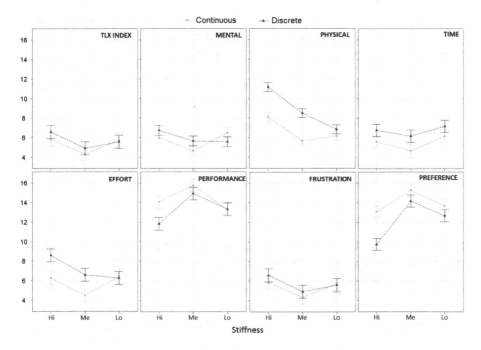

Fig. 5. Summary of NASA-TLX plus preference rating results, including interactions between independent variables. Low values are more positive, except in *Performance* and *Preference*. The error bars represent Fischer's LSD, 95% (overlapping bars are not significantly different in *post-hoc* analysis, 95%).

Table 1. Summary of the 2-way ANOVA analyses conducted for the TLX index and for its sub-categories, plus a *Preference* scale (p values corrected for sphericity using Huynh-Feldt). Levels of significance of at least 95% and 99% are indicated by * and ** respectively.

	Stiffness		Gesture Type		Interaction b/t IVs	
	$F(2,22)$	p	$F(1,11)$	p	$F(2,22)$	p
TLX	2.85	0.103	3.06	0.108	**4.65**	**0.01** **
Mental	**4.68**	**0.02** *	0.34	0.572	**4.53**	**0.036***
Physical	3.75	0.056	**6.82**	**0.024***	**9.03**	**0.005***
Time	1.18	0.316	**6.15**	**0.031***	0.18	0.765
Effort	1.38	0.27	**4.8**	**0.05** *	**4.56**	**0.022***
Performance	**4.16**	**0.043***	1.12	0.313	**3.55**	**0.046***
Frustration	1.99	0.16	0.17	0.687	0.56	0.57
Preference	**4.80**	**0.02** *	**5.79**	**0.035***	**5.00**	**0.017***

The interactions between IVs were statistically significant for the TLX index and for all the sub-categories except *time pressure* and *frustration* (Table 1). Fig. 5 represents these interactions graphically. The origin of the significant interactions in the *TLX index* itself as well as in *effort expended* and *physical demand* was that ratings were more positive with continuous gestures when using high- and medium-stiffness prototypes, but there was no difference between gesture types when using the low-stiffness prototype. The interaction between IVs for the *performance* category had a similar origin, with the difference that ratings were approximately equal with medium and low-stiffness. In all these cases, it was beneficial to use continuous gestures with higher-stiffness prototypes, but the gesture type made no difference when using the lowest-stiffness prototype. In other words, the low-stiffness deformable prototype stood out for being more gesture-type agnostic. In a similar trend, the *mental demand* category presented the singularity that ratings using continuous gestures were more positive (lower) only when using the medium-stiffness RP, but no differences due to the type of gesture were observed with the other two materials.

3.3   User Experience

The subjective user experience was assessed through a quantitative measure of relative preference between conditions, and via semi-structured interviews.

Each NASA-TLX questionnaire was appended with an additional category, called *overall preference*. This category was entirely independent from the TLX method, and was not used for the calculation of the index. Instead, it was a separate scale that the participants also rated at the end of each condition, together with the rest of the NASA-TLX scales, so as to keep the process of evaluation as simple, homogeneous and straight-forward as possible. A two-way, repeated-measures ANOVA test was also performed on these results (see last row in Table 1, and bottom-right graph in Fig. 5). This analysis revealed that both IVs affected the ratings of overall preference statistically significantly. Continuous gestures were preferred over discrete ones, and both medium and low stiffness were preferred over high stiffness in the deformable material. The interaction between the IVs was also significant. The interaction behavior was similar to that observed for *Performance* ratings: continuous gestures were strongly preferred over discrete ones when using the stiffest prototype, but there was no significant gesture preference when using any of the other two materials.

At the end of each experimental session, after all conditions had been conducted, participants were interviewed regarding the user experience in the different experimental conditions. During this interview, participants were asked to choose a single stiffness and type of deformation gesture as their absolute preferred ones. As shown in Fig. 6, medium and low stiffness were equally preferred over high stiffness, and continuous gestures were clearly preferred over discrete ones.

Other comments from the interviews offered further insight into these results. High stiffness was considered good for beginner level, but tiring and laborious, particularly with discrete gestures. Discrete gestures were best performed with medium and low stiffness. The lowest stiffness was pleasant in the hands and it felt very responsive, but it was sometimes described as too sensitive to control with continuous gestures. Some participants commented that discrete gestures were best for short distances and continuous gestures for long distances, just as observed in the performance results.

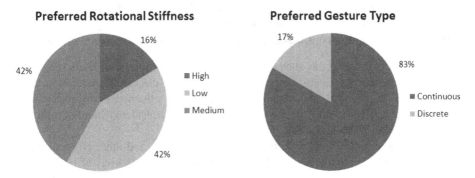

Fig. 6. Preferred rotational stiffness and type of gesture, as selected during the interviews

4   Discussion and Conclusions

The results from this study are valid within the boundaries of the design decisions adopted in the setup: form factor, range of stiffness of the deformable material, navigation tasks by bending and twisting, and discrete/continuous deformation gestures. These were informed design decisions (based on prior literature and on our own iterative piloting) made to encompass a broad and relevant set of use scenarios for current and future DUI design efforts.

For the design space covered in this study, the results showed that the stiffness of the deformable material and the type of deformation gesture had significant effects both on the performance and on the user experience when completing navigation tasks. These variables presented multiple interactions in the quantitative subjective workload and preference measures utilized. Further mining of the results showed that the ergonomics of producing different rotational deformation gestures (namely bending and twisting) modulated the main results in observable ways, pointing towards additional directions in our research agenda.

The main results obtained in this study are summarized in the following points:

- Performance in navigation tasks was significantly worse when they were executed using the prototype with the stiffest deformable material.
- Overall, performance was significantly better with discrete gestures. However, discrete gestures outscored continuous gestures in performance only in short navigation distances. Beyond 4 to 8 units of distance, continuous gestures led to more efficient performance. Future studies should investigate performance behavior in much longer navigation spaces (common in interfaces such as media collections).
- Differences in performance favoring twisting over bending interactions were observed, which could be attributed to ergonomic differences between these gestures.
- The IVs did not have any significant effect on the overall Task load Index. However, in the subjective workload sub-categories, high and medium stiffness were respectively rated least and most favorably. Continuous gestures were rated equally or more favorably than discrete gestures, but never the other way around. With the low-stiffness DUI, continuous and discrete gestures were always rated equally.

- The high-stiffness DUI was particularly disliked (good only for beginners). The low-stiffness DUI was slightly more difficult to control continuously for some.
- Discrete gestures were considered appropriate only for short navigation distances.

To conclude, this research has shown that designing interactions with DUIs (i.e. interactions that require physically deforming material with the hands) requires understanding how mechanical and ergonomic parameters influence performance and user experience. Even within the limited design space considered here, significant influences and complex interactions were observed.

Future work should further investigate the role that these and other physical parameters play in the successful design of interactions with a larger variety of DUIs.

References

1. Vertegaal, R., Poupyrev, I.: Organic User Interfaces. Commun. ACM 51, 26–30 (2008)
2. Ishii, H.: The tangible user interface and its evolution. Commun. ACM 51, 32–36 (2008)
3. Lee, S.-S., Kim, S., Jin, B., Choi, E., Kim, B., Jia, X., Kim, D.: Lee, K.-p.: How users manipulate deformable displays as input devices. In: CHI 2010, pp. 1647–1656 (2010)
4. Ryhänen, T., Uusitalo, M.A., Ikkala, O., Kärkkäinen, A.: Nanotechnologies for Future Mobile Devices. Cambridge Univ. Pr. (2010)
5. The Morph Concept, Nokia Research Center, vol. 2011 (2011)
6. Wightman, D., Ginn, T., Vertegaal, R.: BendFlip: Examining Input Techniques for Electronic Book Readers with Flexible Form Factors. In: Campos, P., Graham, N., Jorge, J., Nunes, N., Palanque, P., Winckler, M. (eds.) INTERACT 2011, Part III. LNCS, vol. 6948, pp. 117–133. Springer, Heidelberg (2011)
7. Gallant, D.T., Seniuk, A.G., Vertegaal, R.: Towards more paper-like input: flexible input devices for foldable interaction styles. In: UIST 2008 (2008)
8. Schwesig, C., Poupyrev, I., Mori, E.: Gummi: a bendable computer. In: Proceedings of the SIGCHI Conference on Human Factors in Computing Systems (2004)
9. Sheng, J., Balakrishnan, R., Singh, K.: An interface for virtual 3D sculpting via physical proxy. In: Proceedings of the 4th International Conference on Computer Graphics and Interactive Techniques in Australasia and Southeast Asia (2006)
10. Murakami, T., Nakajima, N.: DO-IT: deformable object as input tool for 3-D geometric operation. Computer-Aided Design 32, 5–16 (2000)
11. Kildal, J., Paasovaara, S., Aaltonen, V.: Kinetic Device: Designing Interactions with a Deformable Mobile Interface. In: CHI 2012 (2012)
12. Biggs, S.J., Srinivasan, M.A.: Haptic interfaces. In: Stanney, K.M. (ed.) Handbook of Virtual Environments, pp. 93–116. LEA (2002)
13. Chen, J.: Human haptic interaction with soft objects: discriminability, force control, and contact visualization. Dept. Mech. Eng. PhD in Mechanical Engineering (1996)
14. NASA TLX: Task Load Index (2012), http://humansystems.arc.nasa.gov/groups/TLX

An Interactive and Multi-sensory Learning Environment for Nano Education

Karljohan Lundin Palmerius, Gunnar Höst, and Konrad Schönborn

C-Research
Linköping University, Sweden
{karljohan.lundin.palmerius,gunnar.host,konrad.schonborn}@liu.se

Abstract. Swift scientific advances in the area of nanoscience suggest that nanotechnology will play an increasingly important role in our everyday lives. Thus, knowledge of the principles underlying such technologies will inevitably be required to ensure a skilled industrial workforce. In this paper we describe the development of a virtual educational environment that allows for various direct interactive experiences and communication of nanophenomena to pupils and citizens, ranging from desktops to immersive and multi-sensory platforms. At the heart of the architecture is a nanoparticle simulator, which simulates effects such as short-range interaction, flexing of nanotubes and collisions with the solvent. The environment allows the user to interact with the particles to examine their behaviour related to fundamental science concepts.

Keywords: Learning Environment, Nanoscience concepts, Interaction, Multi-sensory, Haptics, Audio.

1 Introduction

Rapid scientific progress in nanoscience suggests that nanotechnology will play an increasingly prominent role in our everyday lives, so learning about phenomena at the nanoscale is becoming increasingly important[1]. Thus, knowledge of the principles underlying nanotechnologies will be required to be harnessed if we are to ensure a skilled industrial workforce. In addition, an awareness of 'nano' is critical for the public to make informed democratic decisions concerning the perceived benefits and risks associated with nanotechnology, as society adapts to the emerging nanorevolution. Research-based educational interventions for exposing learners to nano concepts are urgently required to meet these needs.

This paper describes the development of a virtual educational environment that allows pupils and citizens to directly experience different interactive nanophenomena, ranging from desktops to immersive and multi-sensory hardware platforms. The system includes a simulation of nanoparticles that runs at an interactive rate. Through computational steering, the simulation is connected to direct manipulation by the user allowing for instantaneous feedback about the behaviour and reaction to user input. The simulator includes interaction between nanoparticles as well as intermolecular interaction between nanoparticles and solvent molecules.

C. Magnusson, D. Szymczak, and S. Brewster (Eds.): HAID 2012, LNCS 7468, pp. 81–90, 2012.
© Springer-Verlag Berlin Heidelberg 2012

There are three main contributions of this paper. Firstly, a description of an immersive, multi-sensory learning environment with inherent flexibility and portability between capabilities on different hardware platforms. This aims to provide support for different educational situations, ranging from classroom studies to public exhibitions. Secondly, we present approaches and methods for simulating nanoparticle behaviour at interactive rates. Thirdly, we provide links between the interactive environment and intended learning outcomes.

2   Nanoscience and Educational Perspectives

Nanoscience concerns structures that have at least one dimension in the range of 1–100 nm. At this level of scale, objects manifest radically different physical properties from the macroscopic scale of everyday life[9]. Examples of such contrasts are the inherent *stickiness* of molecules due to attractive intermolecular forces, the drastically reduced influence of gravity in comparison with other forces, and the constant random motion of nano-objects in solution.

2.1   Framing the Problem

The differences noted above are not intuitive for learners, and educational research suggests that pupils have difficulties in attempting to make transitions between different levels of scale, and in particular, grasp the specific scale at which nanophenomena occur[4]. A further obstacle for learning is that the nanoscale is inaccessible to our immediate senses. In addition, a lack of knowledge concerning the basis of nanotechnology has also been observed amongst the public[1].

Visualizations are often necessary for communicating the abstract and non-perceptual nanoscale ideas. Immersive multimodal systems have shown great potential as learning tools for nanotechnology concepts[4]. The notion that learning is connected to our bodily experiences[11] could be exploited by an immersive virtual representations of nanophenomena. Such a system could stimulate learners to integrate embodied knowledge in their construction of a scientific understanding concerning principles that govern the behavior of matter at the nanoscopic scale.

Recent work on learning in virtual environments in a nano-context has focused on letting users interact with simulations of advanced equipment such as atomic force microscopy[5,6]. However, apart from a few examples (e.g. [8]), there are not many available virtual learning environments that actually allow students to interact with representations of nanoscale objects.

For some concepts, we deem that the interactive, multimodal experience of nanoparticle behaviour is essential. However, for other concepts a subset of features may suffice. To facilitate an optimal balance between features and affordability for each purpose, the learning environment is designed to include a set of capabilities that include nanoparticle simulation, 3D computer graphics, interaction and sound, and a high level of portability between different hardware platforms. The interactive capabilities will then be enabled by the platform on which the system is executed. By supporting portability between different hardware platforms, we make it possible to choose between a variety of capabilities.

2.2 Educational Aspects

Key aspects in constructing the understanding necessary for an accurate assessment of both toxicicty and potential benefits of nanotechnology resides in considering the influence of inter-molecular forces, inter-molecular collisions, Brownian motion, as well as adhesion between nanoparticles into aggregates that may lead to sedimentation as gravity becomes the dominating force. To expose the learner to an environment that communicates these aspects, we define two contrasting scenarios: nano-tube aggregation which may be associated with potential toxicity, and nano-particle specificity and increased surface area which may have therapeutic applications. A learners' solving of these scenarios underlies being able to judge and make decisions about the hopes and fears that the nano-revolution brings with it.

At least four actors play a role in the design and implementation of the virtual environment as a platform for user interaction and learning, namely *scientific understanding, task scenarios, actual user interaction* and *interaction design theory*. Conceptualising the structural and interactive dimension of the multi-sensory virtual learning environment requires the simultaneous integration of each of these four components (figure 1).

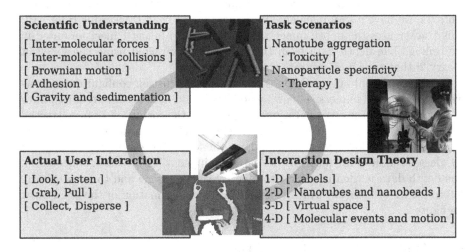

Scientific Understanding

[Inter-molecular forces]
[Inter-molecular collisions]
[Brownian motion]
[Adhesion]
[Gravity and sedimentation]

Task Scenarios

[Nanotube aggregation
: Toxicity]
[Nanoparticle specificity
: Therapy]

Actual User Interaction

[Look, Listen]
[Grab, Pull]
[Collect, Disperse]

Interaction Design Theory

1-D [Labels]
2-D [Nanotubes and nanobeads]
3-D [Virtual space]
4-D [Molecular events and motion]

Fig. 1. Overview of four components underpinning the design and implementation of the multi-sensory nano-technology learning environment

3   Architecture and Core Capabilities

There are two aspects of the learning environment that place hard constraints on the design of the system: it must be flexible in that its core capabilities can be activated and deactivated depending on the hardware platform on which it is run, and all components must be updated at interactive rates. Therefore, multi-threading and modularity were two important design principles.

The learning environment is implemented in H3D API[3], which is a system for implementing multimodal applications with graphics, sound and haptics. The system runs at least two concurrent and asynchronous threads: one controlling the 3D environment, playing sound and displaying graphics, and the other running the nanoparticle simulator. The heart of the system and the most important core capability is the nano simulator displayed in a 3D environment, which is described in detail in section 4.

Other core capabilities are described below. Each defined capability may spawn a separate asynchronous thread that provides its specific functionality to the overall system.

3.1 Immersive 3D Technology

To enable an immersive experience for the learner, our system implements head tracking to calibrate and adjust user's view relative to the position of her/his eyes. This capability can be used together with a 3D TV to present computationally rendered objects in front of the user.

We have previously connected tracking with commercial equipment to H3D API and made the developed package publicly available as open source (H3D Candy/HVR). For the final system to be affordable for schools and other learning contexts, we have also implemented a Kinect-based head tracker for H3D API. This tracker uses the depth image from a downward facing Kinect mounted in the ceiling. The depth data from the Kinect are extracted using the Freenect library[2] that runs in a separate thread.

Some systems only use position tracking to view frustum configuration. However, to get a good immersive view, head orientation data are also required both to correctly direct the eye separation and to obtain the correct offset from tracked position to eye position. To enable high fidelity tracking of head position and orientation from the low quality Kinect data, the following techniques are applied: 3D glasses required for most 3D TVs are equipped with a rectangle geometry. The depth data is then used first to identify the rectangle and to subsequently determine its orientation which can be used as an estimation of the head pose, see figure 2.

3.2 Hand Detection and Interaction

An important feature of interactive learning environments is user action and subsequent system reaction that facilitates the understanding of complex behaviour. In our system, we allow the *grabbing* and *pulling* of nanoparticles so that the user can, for example, see how the particles adhere to each other with different intermolecular force strengths depending on surface area and shape.

We provide the opportunity to reach into the virtual environment by simply using the previously implemented tracking bridge for commercial tracking technology mentioned above, or the haptic hardware support readily available in H3D API. We have also implemented grabbing gestures together with the Kinect-based head tracking.

Fig. 2. The processed Kinect depth image showing simple hand gestures that represent a *grab* (green circles) and the rectangle geometry mounted to the 3D glasses, that provides both position and orientation information about the user's head (green lines)

Using techniques similar to those of [10] we detect a simple grasping gesture where thumb and index finger meet to form a circle, see figure 2. We anticipate that this gesture is simple and intuitive enough for use without much training, and at the same time,it is easy to robustly detect even with low quality data.

3.3 Haptic Technology

An important aspect of our learning environment is its multi-sensory feedback. When haptic technology is available on the hardware platform at hand, the device will be used as input for interaction and to provide force feedback from the simulation. The feedback directly reflects the force interactions between the grabbed particle and the surrounding environment in both inter-particle effects and the interactions with the solvent that give rise to the Brownian motion. Apart from seeing the behavioural response of the particle to the outer disturbance represented by the user action, by also feeling the strength and dynamics of the interacting force, the user will have a much better foundation from which to understand the relationship between the involved effects.

3.4 Audio Technology

Audio feedback is supported by the H3D API and when the underlying platform supports it, real 3D sound using generic Head-Related Transfer Functions (HRTF) will be applied to also give a sense of sound direction. The sound is generated by adding positional sound sources at positions and through parameters determined by the interaction points processed by the nanoparticle simulator.

The audio feedback can be activated to strengthen the sense of interactions provided between particles in the simulation. The sound feedback reflects interaction energy and interaction force. The *interaction energy* is zero when the particles are far apart and at a maximum at the optimal interaction distance. The *interaction force* is zero both when the particles are far apart and when they are at rest at the optimal interaction distance. Thus, the will reflect the restlessness of clusters emitting the sound.

4 Nanoparticle Simulator

The central core technology of the system is the nanoparticle simulator, an engine that simulates the time- and space-scaled behaviour of particles at the nanoscale. There are four main effects that the simulation enacts:

- motion of nanoparticles,
- flexing of nanotubes,
- short-range interactions between particles, and
- interaction with the solvent

4.1 Motion and Dynamics of Nanoparticles

Nanoparticle behaviour can be simulated using a rigid-body approach. However, due to the laws of physics at this scale, special collision and near-collision handling is required. The Open Dynamics Engine (ODE) is a powerful open source system for rigid-body simulation that allows for custom callbacks for collision detection and handling. This makes it possible to adapt to the required physics.

Rigid-body simulators distinguish the *body*, which is the dynamics representation of a particle, from its *shape*, which is its geometrical representation. In the ODE, one body can be assigned many shapes that can reside in different *spaces*. Three different shapes, in three different spaces, are used for each of the particle's bodies. These are explained further in sections 4.3 and 4.4.

The current implementation includes two particle types: nanobeads and nanotubes. The system defines nanobeads using simple spherical shapes, whereas nanotubes are defined by a chain of *capsules* consisting of cylinders with spherical caps. In this simulation we connect the nanotube segments into a chain using what are referred to as *universal joints*. This joint allows bending, but not twisting of the tube.

4.2 Flexing of Nanotubes

Nanotubes do not exhibit free flexing but are rather stiff. We chose to implement this effect by adding a rotational stiffness to all nanotube joints that adds a torque to the joint when its angle deviates for zero. This torque is controlled through a stiffness that is adjusted to allow the flexing behaviour to approximate the rigidity of real nanotubes.

4.3 Short-Range Inter-particle Interaction

We use a truncated Lennard-Jones (LJ) potential, a simple model that approximates the interaction between atoms or molecules, to estimate the inter-particle interactions. The cut-off distance, r_c , is typically set at $r = 2.5\sigma$, where σ can be considered the "size" of the particle. At this distance, the error resulting from the truncation is negligible.

The ODE is used to locate particles that are within the cut-off distance and thus are subject to the force resulting from the LJ potential. To do so, an *LJ cut-off shape* is assigned to each particle body, and set at 2.5 times larger than the size of the particle. The ODE uses space partitioning to speed up the search for these shapes, and subsequently triggers a callback for each intersecting pair of particles, or pair of segments in the case of nanotubes.

To reduce the risk of instability when the particles are in close proximity where the derivative of the LJ potential becomes large, we add a hard constraint so that if two particles come into close proximity, they will collide using the ODE's rigid-body surface collision handling. For this, a *hard LJ shape* is assigned to each particle body, set at the van der Waal surface of the particle. The ODE is then used to search for and apply rigid-body collisions between these shapes.

4.4   Solvent Interaction

Particles suspended in a solvent are constantly colliding with the surrounding solvent molecules. As a result of imbalances between collisions from different directions, the particles will move in a random pattern, known as Brownian motion. Consequently, three important effects must be exhibited by the simulation: 1) the particles must be transported through the solvent in a manner similar or identical to Brownian motion, 2) momentum only increases in a direction if the particle's current momentum in that direction is lower than the momentum of particles in the solvent, and 3) there must be an absense of collisions with solvent molecules in-between adjacent particles that are so close that no solvent molecules between the particles.

It would require a very large amount of processing power to interactively simulate the solvent as particles. Instead, we use a Monte-Carlo approach and simulate discrete collisions at random positions in space. Instead of solvent molecules, we use a single randomized ray, and instead of the particle's surface, we use a larger shape corresponding to the combined size of the particle and the solvent molecule. Although this approach provides us with the same effect, ray–shape intersection is much quicker to estimate than shape–shape intersection.

ODE is used to test the randomized ray against these *solvent collision shapes*. If positive, the ray's relative momentum is transferred to the particle upon collision. Each collision is applied over time to simulate the soft pushing of the solvent molecules.

4.5   Performance

The current performance of the simulator is limited by ODE, which at this point, exhibits serial processing and cannot take advantage of the multi-core technologies. The simulation step used is 10 ms simulation step, so all the physical simulation needs to be performed within this time. To balance the computational requirements against power we adjust the number of rays used to simulate the solvent while maintaining the total amount of momentum.

On our current Intel Core 2 Duo E8500 platform, the simulation uses approximately 7000 rays for ten tubes of five segments each. Alternatively, it uses approximately 9000 rays for 20 beads.

5 Hardware Platforms

The system is designed for high portability and the selection of hardware platforms depending on the learning situation and target concepts. For example, a school scenario might adopt desktop computers for introductory principles and switch to more advanced hardware only for an advanced course on the topic.

We are currently investigating four different hardware platforms, three of which are shown in figure 3. The current focus is on the workbench environment.

(a) The Workbench   (b) The Haptic Workstation (c) The Haptic Workbench

Fig. 3. Three of the target hardware platforms

The desktop environment (not shown) provides 2D graphics and a 2D input device without haptic feedback. This platform will allow for an entry level nano experience. The sound feedback can be rendered in 3D.

The workbench environment uses head tracking in combination with a stereo enabled display to provide an immersive sense of 3D. Our current implementation aims to provide a highly affordable immersive experience, using Kinect for tracking in conjunction with a commercial 3D TV. The interaction with the nanoparticles is colocated with the graphics representations, while the head tracking allows for accurate 3D sound directions.

The haptic workstation environment is a semi-immersive, 3D and haptics enabled version of the desktop environment, see figure 3(b). A stereo enabled screen displays 3D graphics through a mirror providing colocation with a haptic device and interaction. Although 3D sound is less effective in this platform, the haptic feedback provides the sense of intermolecular force dynamics when pulling nanotubes apart.

The haptic workbench environment is a workbench environment equipped with haptic device(s) for force feedback from the interaction with the nanoparticles, see figure 3(c). Here, we have colocated interaction, the haptic sense of forces as well as accurate 3D sound.

6   User Interaction and Learning

Describing the developed virtual environment by applying Crampton Smith's four "dimensions" [7] provides grounded points of departure for implementing the interaction design (see figure 1). With respect to 1-D, our design will use textual labels to denote the types of virtual objects displayed (e.g. "carbon nanotube") as well as textual descriptors of the task scenarios (e.g. "pull the carbon nanotubes apart"). Visual representation of the virtual objects (e.g. nanotubes and nanoparticles) will constitute the 2-D component. Representation of the volume wherein events such as nanotube aggregation in the form of the virtual space afforded to the user will establish the 3-D aspect of the interaction design. Application of the 4-D is manifested by simulating events such as intermolecular adhesion and collisions between nanotubes, in combination with auditory cues to depict aspects such as nanotube *stickiness*.

As exemplified in figure 1, interaction with the virtual environment will take the form of users' multi-sensory experience of performing two tasks related to the benefits and risks of nanotechnology. Performing the tasks requires behavioural and gestural interactions with the system such as looking, listening, grabbing and pulling virtual objects. The direct manipulation interface affords the construction of scientific understanding such as intermolecular forces and Brownian motion. The offered interactive multi-sensory experience might provide the conceptual basis for reasoning around the potential toxic and therapeutic implications of nano-materials.

7   Conclusions

The development of the described system is part of an ongoing project focussed on studying visual and interactive systems for nano education. For this purpose, we have developed a system with several important core capabilities: immersive 3D computer graphics with interactive simulation of nanoparticle behaviour, which is strengthened by audio and haptic feedback when available. This system takes advantage of modern multi-core processors by using asynchronous threads for CPU intensive processing, thereby allowing interactive update rates. It is also designed to run on several different platforms, which enables the utilization of different capabilities depending on the learning situation.

8   Future Work

In commencement of the user data collection phase, the system will be installed in a public arena where people of all ages will be able to explore the principles of nanotechnology. It is in this initial context that we plan to conduct the initial studies on the current qualities of the system and assess further needs by measuring variables such as patterns of user interaction, and any potential changes in the users' attitudes towards nanotechnology, as well as measuring the conceptual understanding related to nanophenomena.

Acknowledgements. This work is supported by the Swedish Research Council (VR) grant 2011-37694-88055-31.

References

1. Batt, C.A., Waldron, A.M., Broadwater, N.: Numbers, scale and symbols: the public understanding of nanotechnology. Journal of Nanoparticle Research 10(7), 1141–1148 (2008)
2. Freenect library, http://openkinect.org
3. H3D API, http://www.h3dapi.org
4. Hingant, B., Albe, V.: Nanosciences and nanotechnologies learning and teaching in secondary education: A review of literature. Studies in Science Education 46(2), 121–152 (2010)
5. Jones, G., Minogue, J., Tretter, T.R., Negishi, A., Taylor, R.: Haptic augmentation of science instruction: Does touch matter? Science Education 90(1), 111–123 (2006)
6. Marchi, F., Urma, D., Marliere, S., Florens, J.L., Besancon, A., Chevrier, J., Luciani, A.: Educational tool for nanophysics using multisensory rendering. In: Proceedings of World Haptics Conference (2005)
7. Moggridge, B.: Designing Interactions. The MIT Press (2007)
8. Persson, P.B., Cooper, M.D., Tibell, L.A.E., Ainsworth, S., Ynnerman, A., Jonsson, B.H.: Designing and evaluating a haptic system for biomolecular education. In: Proceedings of Virtual Reality Conference (2007)
9. Stevens, S., Sutherland, L.A., Krajcik, J.: The big ideas of nanoscale science and engineering: A guidebook for secondary teachers. NSTA Press (2009)
10. Wilson, A.D.: Robust computer vision-based detection of pinching for one and two-handed gesture input. In: Proceedings of the 19th Annual ACM Symposium on User Interface Software and Technology (2006)
11. Wilson, M.: Six views of embodied cognition. Psychonomic Bulletin & Review 9(4), 625–636 (2002)

Augmenting Media with Thermal Stimulation

Martin Halvey[1], Michael Henderson[2], Stephen A. Brewster[2],
Graham Wilson[2], and Stephen A. Hughes[3]

[1] School of Engineering and Built Environment, Glasgow Caledonian University,
Glasgow, G4 0BA, UK
martin.halvey@gcu.ac.uk
[2] School of Computing Science, University of Glasgow, Glasgow, G12 8QQ, UK
0701034H@student.gla.ac.uk, stephen.brewster@glasgow.ac.uk,
gawilson@dcs.gla.ac.uk
[3] SAMH Engineering, 1 Leopardstown Drive, Blackrock, Dublin Ireland
stephenahughes@gmail.com

Abstract. Thermal interfaces are a new area of research in HCI, with one of their main benefits being the potential to influence emotion. To date, studies investigating thermal feedback for affective interaction have either provided concepts and prototypes, or looked at the affective element of thermal stimuli in isolation. This research is the first to look in-depth at how thermal stimuli can be used to influence the perception of different media. We conducted two studies which looked at the effect of thermal stimuli on subjective emotional responses to media. In the first we presented visual information designed to evoke emotional responses in conjunction with different thermal stimuli. In the second we used different methods to present thermal stimuli in conjunction with music. Our results highlight the possibility of using thermal stimuli to create more affective interactions in a variety of media interaction scenarios.

Keywords: Thermal, stimulation, emotion, audio, visual, valence, arousal.

1 Introduction

Thermal stimulation is an emotive and salient feedback channel, but it has yet to be fully investigated. Thermal stimulation has a number of potential benefits for interaction. It can act as an alternative non-visual notification channel for situations that are too bumpy or noisy for vibrotactile and audio feedback. Thermal output is also entirely private; in contrast, vibrotactile feedback can sometimes still be heard or felt by others. It can augment both visual and non-visual displays to add an extra richness to the interaction experience. In particular, in many cases it may be possible to enhance or dampen affective (emotion/feeling) experience, such as in gaming, media or many other fields, as thermal stimulation is said to have an inherent emotional aspect [1]. Indeed, several systems have proposed the use of thermal stimulation as a way of conveying emotion or enhancing affect in users [2-7]; however, none of these systems have effectively determined methods for influencing emotion. Other work by Wilson et al. [8] and Salminen et al. [9] focus on user responses to a thermal stimulus, but do

C. Magnusson, D. Szymczak, and S. Brewster (Eds.): HAID 2012, LNCS 7468, pp. 91–100, 2012.
© Springer-Verlag Berlin Heidelberg 2012

so in isolation, which ignores the possibility of using thermal stimuli to add extra affective richness to interaction. Nakashige et al. [7] presented a first attempt at this by presenting people with images of food and thermal stimuli. They found that in some limited cases thermal stimuli influenced the perception of the images, such as eliciting a feeling of a "loving home" from warm soup. However, their findings were for a very limited range of visual information (familiar warm and cold objects/scenes), as they did not explore the full range of uses for thermal stimuli, either in terms of content (i.e. beyond simply warm/cold objects) or affective response to that content. To overcome these shortcomings in understanding the application of thermal stimuli to alter the affective state of a user we conducted two studies. In the first we presented images which had been mapped to a variety of emotions [10] in conjunction with thermal stimuli. Our aim was to determine if presenting thermal stimuli with visual information could influence the user's affective experience/response. Following on from this, we conducted a second evaluation, where we used some of the temperature-emotion mappings to create different thermal sensations in conjunction with music. Our aim is to compare different thermal presentations for enhancing subjective emotional responses.

2   Related Work

There are a number of prototypes that use thermal stimulation for affect. Gooch [2] constructed a device to provide thermal feedback with the goal of increasing feelings of social presence in remote interactions. His findings indicated that the use of the device significantly increased the feeling of social presence. Hannah et al. [3] proposed a number of prototypes that use mobile devices for interacting with televisions for entertainment. One prototype used thermal stimuli to enhance media browsing by presenting cool stimuli for programs with cold themes and vice versa. Iwasaki et al. [4] present a prototype called the AffectPhone, a system that detects a user's emotional state and conveys this state via changes in the temperature of the back panel of the handset of the other user. Narumi et al. [5] developed the Thermotaxis system, where users are encouraged to explore a physical space using thermal stimuli by using hot and cold spots in the space. Lee and Lim [6] investigate the prospect of thermo-messaging, conveying information with thermal stimuli. Lee and Lim discuss an emotional aspect of thermal stimuli as being one of the benefits, but did not investigate this aspect in detail. As discussed earlier, Nakashige et al. [7] augmented images and a search game with thermal stimuli from adapted computer mice. They found that, in some cases, temperature could enhance emotional feeling when presented with congruent visual stimuli. Williams and Bargh [11] have demonstrated how thermal stimulation can influence perception of others and decision making. Most of these studies are proofs of concept and none discuss the mapping between different stimuli and emotions and, in many cases, do not provide robust evaluations.

To provide a more in-depth understanding of the effectiveness of thermal stimuli, Wilson et al. [8] examined responses to thermal cues in terms of subjective comfort and intensity. While this is useful for designing thermal interfaces, they do not provide guidelines for enhancing media with thermal stimuli. With a focus on emotion, Salminen et al. [9] investigated if thermal stimuli presented to the palm could influence emotional responses when measured with emotion-related subjective rating scales and changes in skin conductance response (SCR). Their results showed that two different methods for presenting warm stimuli elevated the ratings of arousal and dominance, and in some cases that warm and cold stimuli elevated the SCR. These final two studies indicate that thermal stimuli can be used to influence affect. However, these studies investigated thermal stimuli in isolation. As demonstrated by the research prototypes outlined earlier [2-7], thermal stimuli will be used in conjunction with different media e.g. audio, images etc. in the future, so there is a need to understand the impact of thermal stimuli on the perception of and interaction with media.

3   Equipment

For our studies we used a custom controller connected to a two-channel Peltier heat pump (Fig 1)[1]. Peltier heat pumps allow for a high level of control over temperature output and also allow for both heating and cooling from the same pump. Both Peltier devices could be independently controlled via Bluetooth, with the temperature set anywhere within the range of -20°C to +45°C, accurate to 0.1°C.

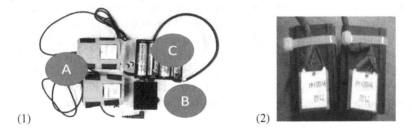

(1)   (2)

Fig. 1. (1)Thermal hardware used in the experiment consisting of microcontroller (B), Peltier stimulators (A, white squares) and battery pack (C). (2) Close up of Peltiers.

4   Evaluation 1: Influence of Thermal Stimuli on Visual Data

4.1   Design and Procedure

The aim of the first evaluation was to investigate the impact of thermal stimuli on visual information designed to evoke emotional responses. In order to provide emotionally stimulating visual information the International Affective Picture System (IAPS) [10] was used. The IAPS was developed to provide a set of normative emotional stimuli for experimental investigations of emotion and attention. From the IAPS collection, we selected 25 images, consisting of 5 images each from 5 emotional

---

[1] Built by SAMH Engineering.

areas selected according to the Russell Circumplex model of affect [12]. This model uses valence and arousal as parameters, valence refers to the please/displeasure continuum, arousal refers to the alertness. The 5 emotional areas we chose were: sad/depressed (low valence/low arousal), nervous/stressed (low valence/high arousal), alert/excited (high valence/high arousal), happy (high valence/low arousal) and calm/bored (low valence/low arousal). We tried to avoid images that could be associated with thermal stimulation e.g. images of warm coffee, etc.

A neutral starting temperature of 32°C was chosen as this is within the defined 'neutral zone' of thermal sensation [8,1]. The skin was adapted to this temperature before each trial session and was returned to it between each stimulus presentation. As thermal perception is bipolar, both warming and cooling stimuli were used. One thermal stimulus intensity point was used: 6°C, meaning the terminal points were 38°C and 26°C; two temperatures that are well removed from the cold and hot pain thresholds. This single intensity point was chosen to ensure that users felt the stimulus [8]. Two different rates of stimulus change (ROC) were used: 1°C/sec and 3°C/sec. Different ROC's were used as a user's perceived magnitude of the sensation is not based solely on the extent that the stimulator changes from skin temperature, but also by the ROC to that end point. For example, the same intensity (e.g. 6°C) will feel subjectively less intense when warmed/cooled at the slower ROC of 1°C/sec, compared to the faster 3°C/sec [8]. Thus different ROC could have an impact on perception of media. Thus a single stimulus consisted of warming or cooling to a set intensity (6°C) and at one of two ROC (1°C/sec or 3°C/sec), for example, warming 6°C at 1°C/sec. Including the 'control' stimulus of not changing the temperature when an image was presented, this meant there were 5 possible stimuli which are no thermal stimulation, warm slow, warm fast, cool slow and cool fast. Each possible thermal stimulus was presented with a single image from each of the 5 emotional spaces. The thermal stimuli were all presented to the Thenar eminence (the bulbous region of the palm adjoining the thumb) of the non-dominant hand. This was chosen as Wilson et al. [8] found it had the highest sensitivity.

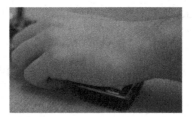

Fig. 2. Thenar placed on Peltiers

Each participant was sat at a desk upon which there was a computer monitor and mouse. The Peltier stimulators lay on the desk in front of the participant, facing up so that the users could lay the Thenar of their non-dominant hand on the stimulators (see Fig 2). At the start of each condition, the stimulators were set to a neutral temperature of 32°C for 1 minute so as to adapt the skin to this temperature. After the adaption period, all 25 images and thermal stimulus combinations were presented in a random order. A stimulus presentation comprised of 10 sec. of thermal stimulus while viewing the image followed by a return to the neutral temperature and at least 20 sec. of adaptation, the image was only present during the thermal stimulus. Once the stimulation was over, two 9-point Likert scales appeared on screen asking the participants to rate the image in terms of intensity (from "weak" to "intense") and pleasantness (from "negative" to "positive"). The independent variables were: rate of change (1°C/sec or 3°C/sec), direction of change (warm or cool), and image emotion (sad/depressed, nervous/stressed, alert/excited, happy and calm/bored). The dependent variables were: subjective intensity (arousal) and subjective pleasantness (valence).

Thirteen participants took part in our evaluation; the majority were staff or students at the University. The group consisted of 10 males and 3 females, with an average age of 28. All were right handed and were paid £6.

4.2   Results and Discussion

A Friedman's analysis of variance by ranks was used to analyse the effect of direction of change (warm and cool), rate of change (1°C/sec or 3°C/sec) and image emotion (sad/depressed, nervous/stressed, alert/excited, happy and calm/bored), with Wilcoxon pairwise comparisons. Table 1 shows the impact of direction on the average valence and arousal values for each of the emotional groups. Direction of change was found to have a significant effect on valence for the excited emotion ($\chi2$ (2)=9.875, p=0.007). Post hoc Wilcoxon T (adjusted alpha = 0.0167) comparisons showed significant differences in the perceived valence between cool and constant (z=2.653, T=83, p=0.008). As well as these significant changes some interesting trends were observed. In general, warm changes result in higher valence and arousal values in comparison with cool, with some exceptions. Also, again with some exceptions, thermal stimulation increases arousal, but decreases valence in comparison with no changes in thermal stimulation.

Table 1. Average, median and standard deviation for valence and arousal for each emotion and direction of stimulation

	Valence					Arousal				
	Bored	Excited	Happy	Sad	Stressed	Bored	Excited	Happy	Sad	Stressed
Warm	6.308	4.692	7.462	3.385	2.346	3.654	6.308	4.308	5.731	6.731
	6.5	4.5	7.5	3	2	3	7	4	6	7
	1.517	2.131	1.449	1.098	1.294	2.190	1.995	2.259	1.710	1.733
Cool	6.154	4.308	7	2.961	2.615	3.462	6.615	3.615	5.346	6.038
	6	4	7	3	2.5	3	7	3	6	6
	1.617	1.892	1.265	1.183	1.359	2.044	1.768	1.551	1.875	1.949
Constant	7.077	6.538	7.538	2.462	2.769	3.154	5.692	2.846	6.154	5.923
	7	4	8	3	3	2	6	2	6	7
	1.320	1.450	1.330	0.967	1.013	2.340	2.250	2.075	1.345	2.431

Table 2 shows the impact of rate of change on the average valence and arousal values for each of the emotional groups investigated. Rate of change was found to have a significant effect on valence for the excited emotion ($\chi2$ (2)=11.878, p=0.003). Post hoc Wilcoxon T comparisons showed significant differences in the perceived valence between 3°C/sec and constant (z=2.816, T=85.5, p=0.005). As well as these significant changes some interesting trends were observed. A comparison of the two ROC shows that they have similar arousal values; however the faster ROC has a higher valence value indicating that it was more pleasant. In comparison with no stimulation, there are mixed results but the ROC does not seem to have as large an impact as the direction of change did.

Table 2. Average, median and standard deviation for valence and arousal for each emotion and ROC

	Valence					Arousal				
	Bored	Excited	Happy	Sad	Stressed	Bored	Excited	Happy	Sad	Stressed
1°C/sec	6	4.346	7.154	3.385	2.769	3.115	6.231	4.385	5.269	6.231
	6	4	7	3	2.5	3	7	4	6	6.5
	1.523	2.190	1.156	1.329	1.366	1.818	1.861	2.041	1.823	1.796
3°C/sec	6.461	4.654	7.308	2.962	2.192	4	6.692	3.538	5.808	6.538
	7	5	8	3	2	3	7	3	6	6.5
	1.581	1.832	1.569	0.916	1.234	2.298	1.892	1.794	1.744	1.944
Constant	7.077	6.538	7.538	2.462	2.769	3.154	5.692	2.846	6.154	5.923
	7	6	8	3	3	2	6	2	6	7
	1.320	1.450	1.330	0.967	1.013	2.340	2.250	2.075	1.345	2.431

5   Evaluation 2: Influence of Thermal Stimuli on Audio

5.1   Design and Procedure

The aim of the second evaluation was to evaluate the impact different methods of presenting thermal stimuli (using some findings from the first evaluation) on listening to music. This evaluation focused on three different emotional areas in the Russell Circumplex model of affect [11]: happy, sad and exciting. Happy and sad were chosen as they are quite different, also many studies of emotion and music have identified happy and sad pieces of music [13,14]. Exciting was chosen as it was most influenced by thermal stimulation in comparison with other emotions in the first evaluation.

The music pieces were chosen based on the dynamics in the music, this was chosen due to its presence in nearly all music. Mohn [15] showed that loud volume is often an identifiable characteristic in happy music, while conversely low volume is an identifiable characteristic of sad music. It was also shown that surprising (close to exciting in the emotional spectrum) was identifiable by ascending dynamics/volume [15]. The happy and sad pieces were all directly used in studies of emotion and music [13,14], while the exciting pieces were chosen to be of the same genre as the others and to match the musical elements in exciting music (as identified above). An excerpt of approximately one minute in length that contained appropriate dynamics was selected from each of the following pieces. The happy pieces were Alfven, 'Midsommervarka' (25s – 1m 23s); Beethoven, 6th Symphony 'Pastoral' (3s – 1m 2s) and Vivaldi, 'La Primavera' (Le Quattro Stagioni Op8 Rv269) (1m 6s – 1m 58s). The sad pieces were Albioni, Adagio Gminor (6m 48s – 7m 52s); Barber, Adagio for Strings (3s – 1m 11s) and Faure, Elegie Cminor Op24 (9s – 1m 14s). The exciting pieces were Beethoven,

Symphony 9 2mvt. 'Molto Vivace' (3s – 1m 21s); Mozart, 'Eine Kleine Nactmusik' 1mvt. Allegro (4s – 57s) and Dvorak, 'Slavonic Dances' Op46 No.1. (1s – 1m 6s).

For each emotion three different presentation styles for the thermal stimulus were chosen. The first presentation type was no stimulus i.e. staying at a neutral temperature. The second was a constant temperature. The final was what we called pulsing, in this presentation mode certain points were chosen in the music track to present thermal stimulus for 10 seconds at a time. 10 seconds was chosen as an arbitrary presentation time. In order to choose when the thermal stimulus should be presented we analysed the dynamics in the audio track. For the happy music the pulse occurred at the highest volume peak; for the exciting pieces the pulses started 3 seconds before their peak, as one of their key classifying elements is their ascending dynamics, crescendos, into peaks; and for the sad pieces the pulse occurred at the lowest volume level. There are other potential presentation styles and parameters we could have chosen, but the intention of the experiment was not to be exhaustive but rather compare the merits of a small set of presentation styles. As well as using different presentation styles for the different music excerpts, different thermal stimuli were also chosen based on the results from the first evaluation. The two non-neutral stimuli will change from either neutral ($30^{0}C$) to hot ($38^{0}C$), if the current emotion of the excerpt is happy or exciting, or neutral to cool if excerpt is sad ($22^{0}C$). It should be noted that we are using larger intensity changes in comparison with the first evaluation, the aim was to evoke more of a response from the participants, these temperatures are still removed from pain thresholds [1]. In all cases the ROC was $3°C/sec$. The task was split into 3 conditions based on emotions, with the order of emotion groups rotated. Participants were seated, in front of a computer monitor, with their non-dominant hand resting on the Peltiers (see Fig 2). Their dominant hand will be used to control the computer mouse to answer questions on-screen. They listened to music using a set of headphones. The skin under the Peltiers was adapted to neutral for 1 minute at the beginning of this experiment. In each emotional block participants heard one of the music excerpts and received a thermal stimulus via one of the presentation techniques. The order of presentation technique and music excerpt was randomised. Once the stimulation was over, two 9-point Likert scales appeared on screen asking the participants to rate the music in terms of intensity (from "weak" to "intense") and pleasantness (from "negative" to "positive"). The independent variables were: presentation type (constant, pulse or none) and music emotion (sad/depressed, alert/excited and happy). The dependent variables were: subjective intensity (arousal) and subjective pleasantness (valence). After the 3 excerpts within an emotional group have been played, the participants were asked to rate their experiences in terms of preference, emotion and stimulation. Nine participants took part in our evaluation; the majority were staff or students at the University. The group consisted of 6 males and 3 females, average age of 22.33 years.

5.2   Results

Table 3 shows the average responses in terms of valence and arousal. None of the differences were found to be significant, but the general trend was that the pulsing presentation style increased arousal across all emotions in comparison with no stimulus. The pulsing also increased reported valence for excited and decreased valence for sad, these emotions are associated with high and low valence respectively. However for happy there is a small decrease in valence. The constant presentation technique increases arousal in the sad and excited categories, but decreases it in the happy category. Constant also increased reported valence for happy and decreased valence for sad, again these emotions are associated with high and low valence respectively. However for excited there is a small decrease in valence. None of these changes in perception were found to be statistically significant.

Table 3. Average and standard deviation for valence and arousal data for each emotion and presentation type

	Happy		Sad		Excited	
	Valence	Arousal	Valence	Arousal	Valence	Arousal
None	6.444	5.778	3.111	6.000	6.778	5.778
	(1.589)	(2.167)	(1.269)	(2.000)	(1.302)	(2.224)
Constant	6.889	5.667	2.667	6.111	6.667	5.889
	(1.167)	(1.732)	(1.000)	(2.315)	(1.732)	(1.691)
Pulse	6.333	6.222	3.000	6.444	7.000	6.778
	(1.732)	(2.108)	(0.866)	(2.007)	(0.866)	(0.667)

The user preferences for the different presentation techniques are shown in Table 4. For exciting pieces of music the participants found the pulse presentation technique to be the most emotive, stimulating and preferable. In contrast, for exciting, the constant presentation technique was found to be the least emotive and stimulating, and as preferable as no presentation. For happy there was very little difference between all presentation styles, although no thermal presentation technique was reported as being more emotive than pulse or constant. Finally for the sad pieces, users had a slight preference for the pulse; no stimulation was the least emotive, but in contrast was reported as being the most stimulating. None of these differences were statistically significant. To gain more insight into user preferences, other feedback provided by the users were analysed. It seemed that previous associations with some of the classical pieces for some users may have caused unexpected results. In particular Barbers Adagio, a sad piece, has been sampled in a modern song so for many it had more positive connotations. Physical separation of the stimuli sources meant that several users felt that there was a disconnection between the audio and thermal (music from headphones, heat on hand). This prevented a unified experience, in some cases causing the thermal stimuli to distract from the music (P7 "I'm very conscious of the thermal sensation. If it were more subtle then perhaps it could --it may have been and I didn't notice it"). In addition some of the participants found the thermal stimuli to be too intense, in particular the warm changes (P3 "didn't really like the hot feeling"; P4 "although being an awesome track, the temperature was too warm and this made the song not very enjoyable"). Despite this many participants enjoyed the thermal sensations in conjunction with the music (P2 "the increasing heat along with the crescendo made it more intense"; P4 "both cold and warm sensation added something to the emotions felt, compared to the normal-temperature sensation").

Table 4. Median rankings for different comparison of presentation techniques

	Con. Exc.	Con. Hap.	Con. Sad	Pul. Exc.	Pul. Hap.	Pul. Sad	Non. Exc.	Non. Hap.	Non. Sad
Prefer	2	2	2	1	2	1.5	2	2	2
Emotive	2.5	2.5	2	1	2	2	2	1.5	3
Stimulating	3	2	2	1	2	2	2	2	1

6 Discussion and Conclusion

This work has highlighted some potential benefits of using thermal stimulation to enhance affect, but has also raised some interesting research questions. Thermal stimulation had an effect on the perceived valence and arousal of both visual and audio media. In general thermal stimulation increases the arousal of media interaction in comparison with no stimuli; also warm stimuli make an interaction more pleasant than cool stimuli. Some feedback from the user evaluations also raised a number of issues which could be investigated in future work. Firstly, some users were very aware of the separation of sources of stimuli, future work will look at the positioning of thermal stimulation to create a more unified experience. Secondly, when the stimulation end point was changed in the second evaluation many participants found the stimuli to be distracting rather than enhancing the experience. A broader range of stimuli should be investigated to match specific media/experiences. Thirdly participants preferred "pulsing" stimulation which matched the content of the media more than constant stimulation. This indicates that matching the stimulation to the content can enhance media more than flat/constant stimulation. More research is needed to match different stimuli with the different content of different media. In conclusion this research has highlighted many future research directions for enabling affective thermal interfaces. Overall this work is an important first step to the realisation of those interfaces and has highlighted the potential of using thermal interfaces to influence the affective perception of multimedia.

Acknowledgements. This research has been funded by the Industrial Members of MobileVCE (www.mobilevce.com), with additional financial support from EPSRC grant EP/G063427/1.

References

1. Stevens, J.C.: Thermal Sensibility. In: Heller, M.A., Schiff, W. (eds.) The Psychology of Touch. Lawrence Erlbaum, New Jersey (1991)
2. Gooch, D.: An Investigation into Communicating Social Presence With Thermal Devices. MSc Dissertation, University of Bath:1-390 (2009)

3. Hannah, D., Halvey, M., Wilson, G., Brewster, S.: Using Multimodal Interactions for 3D TV and Multimedia Browsing. Paper Presented at the 9th International Conference on Interactive Television, EuroITV (2011)
4. Iwasaki, K., Miyaki, T., Rakimoto, J.: AffectPhone: A Handset Device to Present User's Emotional State with Warmth/Coolness. In: BIOSTEC 2010 (B-Interface Workshop), pp. 1–6 (2010)
5. Narumi, T., Akagawa, T., Seong, Y.A., Hirose, M.: Thermotaxis. In: SIGGRAPH 2009, p.1 (2009)
6. Lee, W., Lim, Y.-K.: Thermo-message: exploring the potential of heat as a modality of peripheral expression. Presented at the 28th of the International Conference Extended Abstracts on Human Factors in Computing Systems (2010)
7. Nakashige, M., Kobayashi, M., Suzuki, Y., Tamaki, H., Higashino, S.: "Hiya-Atsu" media: augmenting digital media with temperature. In: Proceedings of CHI 2009, Boston, MA (2009)
8. Wilson, G., Halvey, M., Brewster, S.A., Hughes, S.A.: Some Like it Hot? Thermal Feedback for Mobile Devices. Paper Presented at the ACM CHI Conference on Human Factors in Computing Systems, Vancouver, Canada (2011)
9. Salminen, K., Surakka, V., Raisamo, J., Lylykangas, J., Pystynen, J., Raisamo, R., Makela, K., Ahmaniemi, T.: Emotional Responses to Thermal Stimuli. Paper Presented at the 13th International Conference on Multimodal Interfaces, ICMI (2011)
10. Lang, P.J., Bradley, M.M., Cuthbert, B.N.: International affective picture system (IAPS): Affective ratings or pictures and instruction manual. Paper Presented at the Technical Report A.8. University of Florida, Gainesville, FL (2008)
11. Williams, L.E., Bargh, J.A.: Experiencing physical warmth promotes interpersonal warmth. Science 322(5901), 606–607 (2008)
12. Russell, J.A.: A Circumplex Model of Affect. Journal of Personality and Social Psychology 39(6), 1161–1178 (1980)
13. Baumgartner, T., Esslen, M., Jancke, L.: From emotion perception to emotion experience: Emotions evoked by pictures and classical music. International Journal of Psychophysiology 60(1), 34–43 (2006)
14. Kreutz, G., Ott, U., Teichmann, D., Osawa, P., Vaitl, D.: Using music to induce emotions: Influences of musical preference and absorption. Psychology of Music 36(1), 101–126 (2007)
15. Mohn, C., Argstatter, H., Wilker, F.-W.: Perceptions of six basic emotions in music. Psychology of Music 39(4), 503–517 (2011)

Embodied Interactions with Audio-Tactile Virtual Objects in AHNE

Koray Tahiroğlu[1], Johan Kildal[2], Teemu Ahmaniemi[2],
Simon Overstall[1], and Valtteri Wikström[1]

[1] Aalto University, School of Arts, Design and Architecture, FI-00076 AALTO, Finland
{koray.tahiroglu,simon.overstall,valtteri.wikstrom}@aalto.fi
[2] Nokia Research Center, PO Box 407, FI-00045, Nokia Group, Finland
{johan.kildal,teemu.ahmaniemi}@nokia.com

Abstract. Interactive virtual environments are often focused on visual representation. This study introduces embodied and eyes-free interaction with audio-haptic navigation environment (AHNE) in a 3-dimensional space. AHNE is based on an optical tracking algorithm that makes use of Microsoft-Kinect and virtual objects are presented by dynamic audio-tactile cues. Users are allowed to grab and move the targets, enabled by a sensor located in a glove. To evaluate AHNE with users, an experiment was conducted. Users' comments indicated that sound cues elicited physical and visual experiences. Our findings suggest that AHNE could be a novel and fun interface to everyday resources in the environment such as a home audio system in the living room or a shopping list by fridge.

Keywords: AHNE, Audio-haptic, non-visual, embodied interaction, 3D UI, Reality Based Interaction, augmented reality.

1   Introduction

Augmented-reality (AR) solutions do not disengage the user so radically from the real environment, and they are, for this very reason, more easily used in everyday-life settings, such as in navigation-aid systems [13]. However, they do still pose on the user the challenge of distinguishing real from virtual, as well as fighting occlusion and visual clutter. These challenges, in some circumstances, can get to have safety implications for the user, such as while driving or during pedestrian navigation. Vision is a dominant sense in multimodal interaction [10]. This dominance drives many interactions, such as the interaction with touch displays and varying demands on visual attention. Thus, the more immersive solutions isolate the users from the physical reality [1]. It is also the basis for most haptic illusions that have been proposed to enhance physicality in the interaction with virtual visuals. Some compelling examples of this are found from research in vision-driven pseudo-haptics research [11]. This paper concerns augmenting reality and interacting with virtual objects in ways that are different from the more common vision-driven approach. We

C. Magnusson, D. Szymczak, and S. Brewster (Eds.): HAID 2012, LNCS 7468, pp. 101–110, 2012.

are interested in the audio-tactile augmentation of a user's environment, and in how he/she explores it and interacts with audio-haptic virtual objects. By taking this approach, we intend to free the user's attention from the strong visual focus of other implementations, and instead shift attention towards the auditory and tactile channels, which often are relegated to play subsidiary roles. It could be argued that shifting the attention from visual augmentation to auditory augmentation is simply shifting the problems that visual augmentation presented, such as the confusing overlapping of real and virtual objects. Indeed, some auditory AR setups have led to this kind of ambiguity being reported by participants in studies [12]. However, we hypothesize that when the auditory expression of an object is retrieved through direct manipulation of that object, the coupling between the action and the resulting audio-tactile expression will be obvious and unambiguous for the user. A similar approach for creating a clear mental image of interactively-created auditory representations has been defended in the field of interactive sonification, where interaction is necessary to clearly understand the information space [6].

In our previous work [7,8] we already found that audio and tactile augmentation can separately enrich the perceived physicality of voluntary actions performed with the hands (force input on a surface, in the case of those studies). We implemented interactions that observed the spatial and temporal rules of sensory integration [5]. One goal in the study that we report here is to investigate how the combination of tactile and audio cues can be used to experience virtual objects in a physical empty space, such as in a large room. An additional goal built on our vision of augmenting the user's immediate surroundings and living spaces with interactive audio-tactile objects: a form of augmenting reality with non-visual, audio-tactile objects. Within this interaction model, we wanted to start by observing how users explore a space in search for virtual audio-tactile objects, how they experience and make sense of the objects they find, and in which ways they decide to manipulate them. Our first iteration with AHNE concerned a simplified set of scenarios: a single large space, which contained no other physical objects and where objects could only be anchored to the absolute space. With this setup we conducted an evaluation in which we intended to (i) evaluate our technical implementation, (ii) assess its intuitiveness and perceived affordances, and (iii) observe the exploratory strategies, procedures and patterns of behavior of the participants in our study.

2   System Design and Implementation

The interaction in AHNE happens in a 3D environment and the content is created with the feedback based on audio and haptics [9]. AHNE uses a depth camera (a Microsoft Kinect, sensor bar) to track the movement of the user in that space. Thus, in its current implementation, the system can be used in any space where the Kinect camera is not exposed to strong infrared light. AHNE also makes use of a hand tracking sensor and a vibrotactile-augmented glove with a finger-flexing feature. These components are described in detail in this section.

2.1   System Components

Hand Tracking. Hand tracking was implemented with a Microsoft Kinect Sensor to track the 3D coordinates of user's hands. These coordinates were later sent as OSC (Open Sound Control) messages and processed in Pure Data (Pd) environment.

The Gloves. Gloves were chosen as the interface device to provide haptic feedback to the hands and collect sensor data to return to the system. All of the sensors and actuators were controlled by an Arduino Fio microcontroller and embedded into the gloves (Figure 1). Through the components in the glove, a flex sensor detects grabbing, accelerometer outputs the angle of the hand, a vibration motor creates the haptic feedback and Xbee Series1 module sends all the data wirelessly to Pure Data.

Objects. Figure 1(c) shows the layer structure of the Objects that includes an outer sphere and an inner cube. The Objects can be manipulated, that is, grabbed and moved to a different location. Objects can be also set with a fixed position and size in the space, which can be used as a global-controller mapped with features that can affect the whole system, such as a master volume controller for the related content.

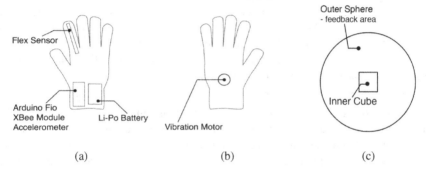

(a)   (b)   (c)

Fig. 1. The electronics, sensors and the vibration motor are embedded in the backside (a) and on the palm of the glove (b). The outer sphere is the feedback area and the inner cube is the actual object that can be manipulated (c).

Audio feedback is activated when the user's hand enters the outer sphere of an object. The feedback sound can be configured to increase in pitch, volume or tempo with increased proximity to the object. When the user actually touches the virtual object, the initial feedback sound stops playing and both the associated sound and the vibration motor in the palm of the glove are activated. If the object is grabbed, the character of the sound changes. The vibration motor remains active until the user's hand moves away from the object. In the experiment, the size of the Inner Cube was 36x36x36cm and the radius of the outer sphere 90cm.

2.2   Sound Design for the Objects

The main audio component of an Object was triggered when the user's hand entered the object's Inner Cube. Audio feedback continued to play as long as the user's hand remained in the cube area. An altered version of this sound was played when the user activated the sensor in the finger by flexing it of closing the hand into a fist. This altered version continued to play as long as the flex sensor remains activated, even if the user moves their hand. This is how the user changed the location of an object. The other component of the audio feedback module was an indicator sound that played when a user's hand was in the Outer Sphere - feedback area, defined for that object. These indicator sounds varied continuously relative to the distance from the user's hand to the Inner Cube, but stopped playing when the user's hand entered the Inner Cube part of the Objects. We implemented three sound objects in the AHNE system for the user-test sessions, which are described below.

1st Object: Wind. For the first sound object, when the user's hand entered the Inner Cube layer the frequency was modulated between 126 Hertz and 554 Hertz, two times per second, by a sine wave, creating an effect similar to a siren. When the user activated the flex sensor, same modulation took place eight times per second generating a more intense sound. The indicator sound for this object, in the Outer Sphere - feedback area, was generated by applying a bandpass filter to a continuous noise source. The bandpass filter had a fairly high Q value, which allowed a narrow band of the noise through and attenuates the other frequencies adding a pitched element to the noise. The center frequency of the filter was correlated to the distance the user's hand was from the Inner Cube layer of the object, increasing as the hand gets closer. The effect sounds were similar to a strong wind, which got higher pitched the closer the user's hand was to the object's Inner Cube layer.

2nd Object: Pulse. The sound for the second object was generated with a method very similar to the first one, however the effect was much more of a pulsing. One difference was frequency of the modulation; another was the shape of the wave that is modulating the frequency. In this pulse sound, the frequency was modulated between 24 Hertz and 392 Hertz. This modulation occurred twelve times a second when the user's hand was in the area and twenty-two times per second when they had activated the flex sensor. It was a pulse sound in which the amplitude of a sine tone was modulated by another oscillator. The result was a pulse very quick at the edge of the Outer Sphere but lowered to a thud near the Inner Cube.

3rd Object: Synth. The third sound object was generated by simple frequency modulation. The modulation index and the amplitude envelope of the sound were controlled by a sawtooth wave, which was slower at six Hertz when a hand was in the Inner Cube and the little bit quicker eight Hertz when the flex sensor was activated. The indicator sound for this third object was slightly detuned, sawtooth waves, enveloped with a sine wave. The result was again pulsing, but reminiscent of a classic cheesy synth sound. With this indicator both the pitch and the rate of the pulses increased as the hand approached the Inner Cube.

Other Sound Cues. A clicking sound was associated with the activation of the flex sensor. A sample of a short, sharp, noisy sound was triggered when the first finger was curled and a second, similar, but slightly softer and lower pitched, sample was triggered when the finger was extended again. The third of these utilitarian sounds was also a short sine tone in this case 70 ms at 200 Hertz. The amplitude enveloped for all these tones had short attacks or onsets and longer decays making them more percussive and easier to associate with the moment they were triggered.

In general, the objects could be freely placed anywhere in the space, and the sound of an Object stopped playing when it was dropped to a new location and the user moved away from it. If an Object was placed inside *the Bubble* area, it continued to play even after the user moved away. This alternative control possibility enabled certain events to happen continuously during any moment of the interaction.

3   Evaluation

We wanted to know more about user expectations with AHNE, including the exploratory strategies and procedures when interacting with the system components. We also wanted to evaluate how intuitively the affordances of the Object interfaces are perceived by users with different background. We were interested in observing the relational descriptors that appears when the user interacts with the virtual objects and the empty space. For that purpose the AHNE system was set up. Three different sound objects and a bubble were placed in the virtual space in fixed locations. Objects were placed apart so that the sounds would not overlap in the beginning of the test.

3.1   Experiment Design

A group of nine participants was recruited for this study (6 male and 3 female, aged between 23 and 38). They were students or researchers of Aalto University. The test users had different levels of familiarity with Microsoft Kinect based systems, ranging from completely naïve to having used it for their own design or artistic projects. No particular instructions or task was given before the experiment. We wanted the user to explore the space freely while thinking aloud (Figure 2a).

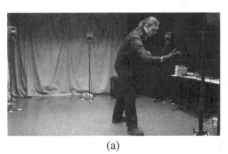 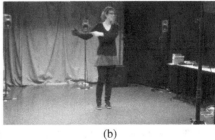

(a)   (b)

Fig. 2. Participant's interactions, exploring the space (a), describing the object she found (b)

Experiment Procedure. The participant was asked to put on the interactive glove, calibrate to the Kinect and then explore the space freely while thinking aloud. No additional information was given about the setup and the interactions. If the user was silent for a long time, the experimenter asked encouraging questions, such as: "*Can you explain what you are doing?*" "*What do you think is happening at the moment?*" "*How would you describe that object?*"

The aim of this study was to encourage participants to express their impressions freely. The word *object* was chosen in the third question so that the user would be more inclined to talk about the tangible and physical properties that they experienced. Clarifying questions were also asked when necessary. Halfway through the 15-minute test, the concept of objects was introduced to the users. Hints about different possible interactions were also provided, if it was observed that the participants could not discover them by themselves. More hints were given, if necessary, so that each user was able to at least find one object and move it (Figure 2b). Each participant was interviewed to gather information about his or her subjective experience.

4   Results

During the experiment, the subjects were asked to explore the space and talk about what they experience. Thus, the outcome of the experiment session consisted of quantitative data of successful interactions with the objects and qualitative descriptions related to their experiences. These are analyzed separately below.

4.1   Quantitative Findings

In the quantitative analysis of the experiment we counted each time a user touched an object without grabbing or moving it as a find and each time a user moved an object as a move. Figure 4 shows number of times users physically interacted with all the sound objects before and after they have been introduced with concept of Objects.

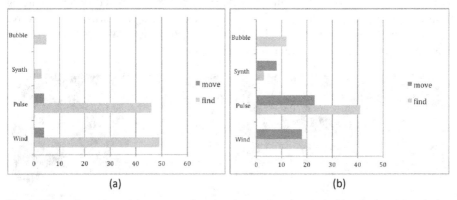

Fig. 3. The total number of times users found and moved each sound object before (a) and after (b) they were introduced with the concept of the Objects

Before information on Objects was given eight of the nine users found the Pulse object a total of 46 times, and two users moved it a total of four times. The Wind object was found by seven users and 49 times, grabbed by two users a total of three times, and moved by two users a total of four times. The Synth object was found by two users a total of three times, it was not grabbed or moved at all. The Bubble object could not be moved, but one user found it a total of 5 times.

4.2   Qualitative Analysis and Main Findings

Objective observation and also subjective comments and ideas from the users, provided flexibility for us to apply a qualitative analytic method for analysis. The thematic analysis method allowed us to establish a certain thematic framework, informed by qualitative answers to the *think aloud* process and interview questions [2]. After we made ourselves more familiar with the collected data, some common issues emerged from the respondents; the limitations of the size of the objects, emotional responses to the audio feedback, the description for the intended interaction, characteristics of the sounds and objects, etc. Looking at these responded items allowed us to identify main themes for the practice of interaction happened during the user-test experimentation: "Confusion and Surprises", "Exploratory Affordances" and "Emotional Experience of the Interaction". Defining these main themes also allowed us to organize responses and comments thematically, eliciting a potential narrative that was not prescribed by the design of the user-test. Related themes became points of discussion within the context of thematic analysis method.

Confusion and Surprises. Confusion and Surprises reflects the range of responses we collected when we asked users to describe the objects. This theme is identified with the perceived qualities of the virtual objects. Confusion is mostly linked to the responses about the shape or size of the objects. At the same time there were number of responses that raised surprised expressions from unique identification of objects:

"Object is very tiny, like a sphere with dust around it" (#3)
"Object is small like a ball"(#9)"I wanted to visualize the shape of objects"(#4)
"It is not an object it is a field" (#5) "Handle" (#9) "Confused" (#1) (#2)
"Nothing in my hands, but I get a feeling of holding it" (#5)
"Trying to catch the sound" (#2) "Invisible objects almost like sculpture" (#2)
"You can take it and move it to somewhere (#1)

Confusion and Surprises might be considered as results of sequences of exploration over time. In the beginning when users asked to explore the space, with no further information about the Objects, they could not find any meaning in it. Confusion reflected a sort of being in an uncomfortable situation for the beginning of the exploration. When some users began to engage with the AHNE system, they also began to identify their experience through their interaction. Confusion evolved towards sort of surprises. In order to imagine new interaction design strategies that could allow AHNE to fulfill this potential, it is useful to consider the ways in which exploration have been reflected by the user's responses.

Exploratory Affordances. While it might not be easy to compare form factor notion of objects in AHNE with some other design objects, we still could identify a potential usage paradigm through the Exploratory Affordances theme raised from the user comments and responses. Apart from the initial movements, typically similar to searching an item in the dark, the functional features of the objects were perceived and utilized by the users when they involved more with exploratory competence. Calm and organized movements followed by patterns to map the space and finding the objects resulted in types of interaction to grab and move the objects.

> "The best part was when I could move the object, then I could interact with it"(#5)
> "I realized quite fast that this gesture (grasp) was to take it with me" (#9)
> "Aha! There are two objects next to each other" (#7)
> "The small thing was more significant because of the vibration and it was more valuable because it was small" (#4)
> "Now the vibration happens here, so I moved invisible object to this location" (#2)
> "Did I grab it? If it is still vibrating then I guess I did." (#8)
> "And when it was vibrating I suppose that means I was holding the object" (#7)

The thematic framework of Exploratory Affordances suggests something we know about the interaction in AHNE; while it centralizes the embodiment in the heart of the interaction it also enables users to create meaning through exploring mutually engaged interaction in natural environment. This is very much similar to Dourish's notion of embodied interaction [3]. Not many interactive systems will open up exploratory affordances for the interaction with their creativity products, nevertheless many designed interaction solutions simply too limited, and make their presence too known to the user, to allow for a known interaction flow.

Emotional Experience of the Interaction. Emotional Experience formulates a type of relationship appeared between the user, the sound objects and the empty space. User comments reflect unique emotional states, when metaphors were also used to identify their experience.

> "I'm in a sound bubble. It is almost dragging me"(#3)
> "Emotionally it was jolly"(#5) "I feel like I should see objects of sound" (#3)
> "I'm kind of reaching a glass ceiling (found bubble)" (#9)
> "I feel like playing hot and cold" #(8) "I'm feeling warmer, warmer, warmer" (#7)
> "It is like being blindfolded" (#8)

While it was not in our intention to design certain interaction elements to evoke certain emotions, emotional context of everyday life grounded users to express themselves throughout the physical and bodily experience of interaction in AHNE. Embodiment offers a way of explaining how we create meaning from our interactions with the everyday world we inhabit [3]. Embodied interaction with ubiquitous objects can create our experience of the world, which depends on our bodies both physically and biologically [4]. The user responses that brought up the thematic framework of Emotional Experience indicates that experience with AHNE is a natural everyday form of interaction, it opens up new worlds of excitement and surprises.

5   Discussions

The user responses that brought up the thematic analysis indicate that the experience with AHNE could merge with other natural interactions in a physical environment.. Coupling between actions and the resulting audio-tactile expression was unambiguous for the users. Moreover, users created meaning from the virtual audio-tactile objects they found in the space and engaged with the AHNE environment throughout their natural actions. The users' spatial and relational coordination had significant influence in the decisions they make for their following actions and also in the way they attach meaning to them. The qualitative findings of the experiment also hinted that the virtual objects acquired physical properties similarly as in our previous study [8]. The participants were visualizing the virtual objects based on how the sound changed with the hand movements. For example, expressions such as 'hot', 'cold', 'sculpture', 'dust' or 'small ball' suggest that the system might have evoked pseudo-haptic experiences [7], which should be further investigated. The virtual and the real merged in a balanced way in AHNE as users did not find themselves disengaged in any of them. Not only the way they described the objects in the space but also when they described their emotions or experience with the objects, they suggested everyday life metaphors rather than abstract descriptions. This clear distinction between the virtual and the real should be confirmed in future AHNE spaces that include more complex combinations with real objects. None of the participants faced any major problems exploring the space and interacting with the virtual objects. A few of the users mentioned that they looked for some type of visual cues during the experiment.

User expectations showed that they were more inclined to explore the interaction when the audio responses were borrowed from daily life or had more organic characteristics. The result of our quantitative analysis also supports this finding (Figure 4). For this experiment we designed sounds with no specific characteristics or content other than just being objects. However, the modular structure of AHNE gives possibility to further design sounds with regard to the context of the interaction.

6   Conclusions and Future Work

Non-visual 3D interfaces provide alternative and challenging design solutions for virtual-reality and augmented reality systems. This paper introduced a study that explored embodied and eyes-free interaction with an audio-haptic navigation system. This study showed that AHNE offers opportunities for real-world augmented reality solutions that do not have to rely on visual augmentation. Thus, it presents interactive audio-tactile augmentation as a promising alternative to visual-augmentation.

It is important to consider how to improve the design of the system in order to move closer to our vision presented in this paper. A natural step forward would be to investigate the pure efficiency of the interaction, for example altering the size and auditory properties of the objects and study how they influence the object selection time. We aim to further develop this first implementation of the system by utilizing it in a more complex environment and for a specific use case. Thus, we intend to implement AHNE as a musical controller in a performance context, which will lead our next steps in this line of research.

Acknowledgements. This research is a part of New Interaction Solutions project funded by the Finnish Funding Agency for Technology and Innovation TEKES and steered by Nokia Research Center. This work is also supported by the Academy of Finland (project 137646).

References

1. Azuma, R., Baillot, Y., Behringer, R., Feiner, S., Julier, S., MacIntyre, B.: Recent advances in augmented reality. IEEE Computer Graphics and Applications 21 (2001)
2. Braun, V., Clarke, V.: Using Thematic Analysis in Psychology. Qualitative Research in Psychology 3(2), 77–101 (2006)
3. Dourish, P.: Where the Action is: the Foundations of Embodied Interaction. MIT Press, Cambridge (2004)
4. Fallman, D.: In romance with the materials of mobile interaction: a phenomenological approach to the design of mobile information technology. Doctoral thesis. Umeå University, Sweden: Larsson & Co:s Tryckeri (2003)
5. Holmes, N.P., Calvert, G.A., Spence, C.: Multimodal Integration. In: Binder, M.D., Hirokawa, N., Windhorst, U. (eds.) Encyclopedia of Neuroscience. Springer (2008)
6. Hunt, A., Hermann, T.: The Importance of Interaction in Sonification. In: Proc. of International Conference on Auditory Display, ICAD (2004)
7. Kildal, J.: 3D-Press: Haptic Illusion of Compliance when Pressing on a Rigid Surface. In: Proc. of ICMI 2010. ACM (2010)
8. Lai, C.-H., Niinimaki, M., Tahiroğlu, K., Kildal, J., Ahmaniemi, T.: Perceived Physicality in Audio-Enhanced Force Input. In: Proc. of ICMI 2011. ACM (2011)
9. Niinimäki, M., Tahiroğlu, K.: AHNE: A Novel Interface for Spatial Interaction. In: Proc. of CHI 2012 Extended Abstracts on Human Factors in Computing System. ACM (2012)
10. Pick, H.L., Warren, D.H., Hay, J.C.: Sensory conflict in judgments of spatial direction. Perception & Psychophysics 6(4), 203–205 (1969)
11. Pusch, A., Martin, O., Coquillart, S.: HEMP-hand-displacement-based pseudo-haptics: A study of a force field application and a behavioural analysis. Int. J. Hum.-Comput. Stud. 67(3), 256–268 (2009)
12. Härmä, A., Jakka, J., Tikander, M., Karjalainen, M., Lokki, T., Hiipakka, J., Lorho, G.: Augmented reality audio for mobile and wearable appliances. J. Audio Eng. Soc. 52(6), 618–639 (2004)
13. Rohs, M., Schöning, J., Raubal, M., Essl, G., Kruger, A.: Map navigation with mobile devices: virtual versus physical movement with and without visual context. In: Proc. of ICMI 2007. ACM (2007)

Towards an Objective Comparison of Scanning-Based Interaction Techniques

Benjamin Poppinga[1], Martin Pielot[1], Wilko Heuten[1], and Susanne Boll[2]

[1] OFFIS – Institute for Information Technology, Germany
{Benjamin.Poppinga,Martin.Pielot,Wilko.Heuten}@offis.de
http://www.offis.de/
[2] University of Oldenburg, Germany
boll@informatik.uni-oldenburg.de
http://medien.informatik.uni-oldenburg.de/

Abstract. The direction where a user points a mobile phone to can be measured with the phone's integrated compass. Pointing over time and with varying direction is often referred to as "scanning", which is an emerging interaction technique and increasingly applied in the field of mobile navigation and orientation. Because there is no need to look at the screen while scanning, often haptic or audio feedback is used. In fact there exist several different scanning-based interaction concepts. However, until now it is impossible to analyse and compare these techniques systematically to identify the best concept for a certain scenario. In this paper we investigated how our own Tactile Compass scanning technique has been used in a field study. Based on our observations we identified a set of measures, which we propose to become a standard set for the analysis and comparison of scan-based interaction techniques. We further argue that our contribution may be beneficial for the creation of guidelines and support designers in selecting a proper scan-based interaction technique.

1 Introduction

Today's smart phones often come with a digital compass, which allows to measure the device's heading. In situations where the user holds the phone in his/her hand, the device heading equals the pointing direction of the user (see Figure 1). Pointing over time and with varying direction is often referred to as *scanning*. Scanning is an emerging, often whole-body interaction technique. The actual scanning can be done without spending visual attention on the device, which facilitates the use of, e.g., audio or haptic feedback. The interaction technique is most prominently used in the domain of user orientation and navigation, e.g., [2,10,7]. There it is applied to, e.g., convey the direction to the next way point of a route by, e.g., presenting a tactile cue once the user points in the right direction. It is argued that this interaction technique supports exploratory navigation [9].

The design space for scanning-based interaction concepts is huge, as it has to be decided which feedback is presented for which angles. Consequently, several

C. Magnusson, D. Szymczak, and S. Brewster (Eds.): HAID 2012, LNCS 7468, pp. 111–120, 2012.
© Springer-Verlag Berlin Heidelberg 2012

Fig. 1. Scanning is a novel interaction technique and often used in the domain of pedestrian orientation and navigation systems. A user holds a mobile phone almost parallel to the ground, points it to varying directions, and receives feedback.

different multi-modal interaction concepts have been investigated and published. Most of the concepts come with studies, which show that a scanning-based interaction concept is, e.g., less distracting or more efficient than a traditional interaction technique like a map [7]. More rarely, scanning-based interaction concepts are compared against each other or with other novel techniques. Unfortunately, most studies and comparisons use different, imprecisely defined measures to assess the advantages and disadvantages of the individual interaction concepts. Until now there is no standard test to analyse the qualities of a certain scanbased interaction concept. Consequently it is hard for a researcher to relate a novel scanning-based interaction technique to existing ones. Further, it is impossible for an application designer to assess which scanning-based interaction concept is best suited for a certain purpose or scenario.

In this paper we investigate the essential characteristics of a scan interaction and derive an initial set of measures for the objective analysis and comparison of different scanning metaphors. To do so we recorded the scanning behaviour of 15 study participants, which have been testing our own Tactile Compass scan interaction concept and a map as comparison. We used the logging observation method to ensure that only objective measures, i.e., sensor data, were recorded. The identified set of measures covers the frequency and duration of a scan event, the walking speed while scanning, and which angle span is covered. We argue that this set allows researchers and designers to do a technical, low-level comparison of different scanning-based interaction techniques. We further claim that some measures can give initial indications how, e.g., intuitive, physical or mental demanding a scanning technique is.

The paper is structured as follows. In Section 2 we discuss the related work on scanning interaction techniques and the comparison of these. Section 3 describes the PocketNavigator software, which is a pedestrian navigation application, and our understanding of the scanning metaphor. We used this application with three different conditions to conduct an experiment and record interaction data. We report our observations and discuss our set of standard measures in Section 4. We summarize our findings and illustrate for what the standard set of measures can further be useful for in Section 5.

2   Related Work

Robinson et al. used a scanning-based interaction technique to browse the environment for geo-located content [10]. Tactile feedback is received, if content has been discovered in a scan movement. They found that participants felt familiar with the scanning technique from the beginning and mostly interpreted the feedback while walking. They used the scan duration as measure for the effectiveness of finding content.

Pielot et al. introduced the PocketNavigator, which comes with vibro-tactile navigation support [5]. In a first study they compared the concept with a map and measured the task completion time, disorientation events, and distractions from the environment [7]. In a follow-up study [6] they extended their measures by navigation errors, occurred orientation phases, and by measuring the overall walking speed. They further discuss the task completion time more detailed and report total scan and interaction times. They argue that future work is needed to investigate if this technique can be made more intuitive.

Magnusson et al. [3,2] used audio feedback to indicate whether a user is pointing at the correct direction. Varying angles, ranging from 10° to 180° have been studied. The time to reach the destination, i.e., task completion time, has been used as effectiveness indicator. They found that a narrow 10° angle and wide 180° angle lead to rather long completion times. For exact track following 30° to 60° are recommended. If low cognitive load is important, angles between 60° and 120° should be chosen. They further report about different scan techniques, i.e., wrist flex, arm scans, and whole body rotation.

Rümelin et al. [8] compared their vibro-tactile navigation system NaviRadar with the PocketNavigator and regular spoken instructions in an outdoor study. To compare the systems they measured disorientations, i.e., stopping for more than 2 s, and navigation errors, i.e., travelling in an incorrect direction for more than 5 m.

As the related work shows, scan-based interaction techniques are typically evaluated or compared in a case-by-case field experiment. This is sufficient to show the effects of a novel technique in a real context. However, until now almost no technical measures are reported, which would allow a structured side-by-side comparison of interaction techniques. We aim to fill this gap with the proposal of a set of standard measures.

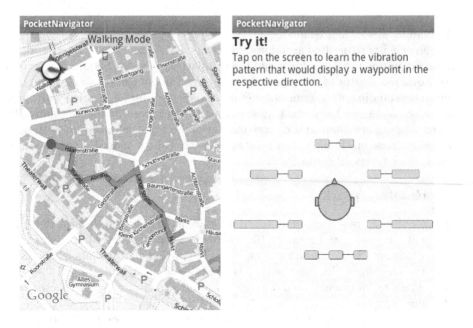

Fig. 2. The PocketNavigator is a pedestrian navigation application, which we used as apparatus for our study on scanning behaviour. These screenshots show an early release of the application, which we used during the study.

3   Background: The PocketNavigator

The PocketNavigator[1] is a pedestrian navigation application similar to Google Maps Navigation [5,7]. It shows the user's location on a visual map and can calculate a route to an arbitrary destination nearby (see Figure 2). One of the essential features of the application is that it is able to convey the direction to a route's next way point by vibration patterns. If the way point is ahead, two vibration pulses of equal duration are presented. If the way point is on the left the first pulse's duration is increased depending on how far left the point is. Accordingly, the right pulse's duration is increased if the way point is on the right. If the way point is approximately behind the user, three short vibration pulses of equal duration are presented. The concept is labelled *Tactile Compass* and visualized in Figure 2.

The application supports two different operation modes. The scanning mode is enabled if the roll and pitch angles of the mobile phone, which can be derived from the accelerometer, are between $-16°$ and $16°$, i.e., the device is held almost parallel to the ground. In scanning mode the device's compass is used to determine the direction to the next way point. The pocket mode is enabled if the device is not in scanning mode. Then the GPS heading is used to determine the direction to the next way point. For this paper only the scanning mode is

---

[1] http://www.pocketnavigator.org/, last visited July 4, 2012.

of relevance. In this paper the PocketNavigator application serves as apparatus for our sensor-based observations to derive the measures on how to define a scan interaction. For an in-depth evaluation and discussion of the different interaction techniques, please read our earlier papers, e.g. [7].

4   Field Study

We conducted a user study to record a typical set of scan movements in the field. 15 volunteers (8 females) participated in our study. The participants were aged from 20 to 29 years (mean 23.6, sd 2.5). Thirteen participants were university students, two were part- or full-time employed.

We used a HTC Dream smart phone, which was running the PocketNavigator application as described above. The study was conducted in the city centre of Oldenburg, a city with about 160,000 inhabitants. We modified the software in a way that several sensor values (i.e., accelerometer, compass, GPS) were continuously saved to the device's memory card.

We decided for a within subjects, i.e., repeated measures, design. Each participant was asked to walk three pre-defined routes of approximately equal length (i.e, about 500 m, containing 10-11 way points) and complexity (i.e., number of decision points, like crossings). For each route one of three conditions was assigned: *tactile only*, *map only*, and *combined*. In the *tactile only* condition, the map was not shown to the user (i.e., a black screen was shown instead) and only tactile feedback was available. In the *map only* condition, the map was shown and no tactile feedback was provided. In this condition the map was by default rotating, i.e., aligning to the user's heading. The rotation of the map could be turned off by the participant, which resulted in a north-up oriented map. We also had a *combined* condition, where tactile and map feedback were both available. To cancel out potential sequence effects, we counter-balanced the conditions.

Initially we asked each participant to sign an informed consent. Before we started with the study we made the participants familiar with the device and our navigation software. We explained all the functions and the participants were able to explore how the device behaves in various situations. On a short training route we answered remaining questions. We particularly emphasized that the participants can grasp, hold and interact with the device as ever they like. We started the study with one of the three conditions enabled. The experimenter followed each participant and video recorded them. We did not assist or influence the users during the actual navigation and orientation task. Once a participant reached the destination of a route, the experimenter changed the condition and the user was then able to go on with the navigation. At the final destination we conducted a brief semi-structured interview, where we asked the participants about their subjective impressions on the different interaction methodologies. Finally, we thanked each participant and handed an USB stick as a reward for participation.

4.1 Filtering and Data Preparation

During the study, the mobile phone logged most of the available sensor data. Most important for this study, GPS location, three dimensional acceleration and the compass heading over time were recorded. For the actual analysis we first converted the acceleration values into roll and pitch angles. We then extracted what we refer to as *scan event*, i.e., if the user is actually doing a scan interaction. By definition a scan event starts, once the roll and pitch angles are between $-16°$ and $16°$. We removed the first second of the scan event, as here sensor values are probably imprecise. A scan event ends, if these angles are exceeded for more than 3 s. To cover only real and intended scan interactions we excluded scan events with a duration of less than 1 s and more than 120 s. We argue that the remaining data set covers only intentional scan interactions. The filtering was applied to all conditions in an equal manner.

Table 1. An overview on all identified measures, their values for our exemplary study, and their potential impact on the user

Measure	Tactile	Map	Combined	Potential Impact
Frequency	16x	13.5x	17x	Physical demand, context switches
Duration	21.05 s	17.35 s	18.87 s	Physical demand, mental demand, intuitiveness
Speed	0.66 m s^{-1}	0.93 m s^{-1}	0.71 m s^{-1}	Efficiency, mental demand, training level
Angle Span	136°	106°	122°	Physical demand, conspicuousness, insecurity

4.2 Scan Frequency

Based on our data set we investigated how often a user scanned. This measure is named frequency and is already used as measure how attentional resources are spend [4]. In the *tactile only* condition scanning means that the user made use of the higher precision of the compass and therefore perceived more responsive and accurate tactile feedback. In the *map only* condition scanning means that the user was probably looking at the display. In the *combined* condition it is unclear, whether a user relied on tactile feedback or was watching the screen.

We found that in the *tactile only* condition a user scanned approx. 16.0 times in average. For the *map only* condition a user scanned 13.5 times, while in the *combined* condition 17 times. Given the complexity of the route that means that a user scanned every 31.25 m (*tactile only*), 37 m (*map only*), or 29.5 m (*combined*). A conducted ANOVA omnibus test indicated that no significant differences can be found ($F(2, 42) = 0.71$, $p = 0.50$).

Each started scan interaction means a context switch, i.e., the user starts to pay more attention to the mobile device and less attention to the environment. Obviously the context switch itself and the following scan action takes time.

Therefore, the scan frequency is a very efficiency- and performance-critical measure. We further observed that users are most likely performing a scan movement if they feel insecure on how to proceed in the way finding/navigation task. Thus, scan frequency is an indicator on how often a user needs reassurance, probably because of insecurity.

4.3 Scan Duration

We also investigated the scan durations and found that for the *tactile only* condition, an average scan event took 21.05 s. For *map only* it took 17.35 s and in the *combined* condition 18.87 s. A conducted ANOVA indicated no significant differences between the three conditions ($F(2, 694) = 1.30$, $p = 0.27$).

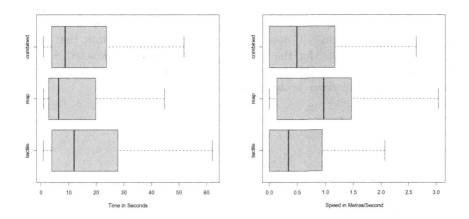

Fig. 3. Scan events in the *tactile only* condition take 21.05 s in average. The average walking speed is, compared to the *map only* condition, significantly lower.

The duration of scan events is an important characteristic of an interaction technique. We assume that the longer a user scans the greater the physical demand is. Further, the duration could give insights on how intuitive a technique is. I.e., a short scan duration could be an indicator for an intuitive technique. Missing intuitiveness means that a user has to actively think about what is perceived, which could be interpreted as an increased mental demand.

4.4 Walking Speed

As shown by other papers, the walking speed is an interesting measure not only for pedestrian navigation [1]. We found that the walking speed in the *tactile only* condition was $0.66 \, \mathrm{m\,s^{-1}}$. For the *map only* condition the speed was $0.93 \, \mathrm{m\,s^{-1}}$, while it was $0.70 \, \mathrm{m\,s^{-1}}$ for the *combined* condition. A conducted ANOVA ($F(2, 694) = 5.53$, $p < 0.01$) and a Bonferroni-corrected post-hoc t-test showed that the walking speeds for the *combined* and *tactile only* condition are both significantly lower than for the *map only* condition ($p < 0.05$ and $p < 0.01$).

We observed that a user often continues to walk while scanning. Thus, the walked distance over time, i.e., walking speed, is also a criteria to characterize a scan interaction technique. We argue that if a user walks, compared to a non-scanning situation, significantly slower, this could be an indicator for the induced mental demand of the scanning-based interaction technique. We further argue that this value might be an indicator on how trained a user is to the interaction technique.

4.5   Covered Angle Span

We further investigated the span, i.e., the overall covered angle, of a scan event (see Figure 4). We found that an average scan motion in the *tactile only* condition spans 136°. For the *map only* condition we observed 106° and for the *combined* condition 122° in average. Compared to the *map only* condition that makes a difference of about 30° for the *tactile only* condition. A conducted ANOVA ($F(2, 694) = 4.17$, $p < 0.05$) and post-hoc Bonferroni-corrected t-test ($p < 0.05$) indicate that this difference is significant.

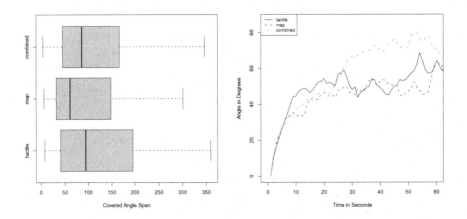

Fig. 4. When compared to the *map only* condition the angle span is significantly wider than in the *tactile only* condition (left). Within the first 10 s of an average scan event the device is moved rapidly, after that the angle remains almost unchanged (right). Note that less scan events contributed to the average angle for higher durations. Therefore, the impact of individual scan events becomes greater.

We analysed how the scan angle varies over time. To make the following analysis independent of the direction of scanning, we used the absolute value for each recorded angle. We found that the average angle dramatically changes in the first 10 s of a scan event from 0°, i.e., straight ahead, to about 50° for the *tactile only* and *map only* conditions, and about 70° for the *combined* condition. After the initial increase, the angle mostly remained unchanged.

A broad angle means that the user has to turn significantly towards left or right. At a certain point the user is unable to cover this angle with wrist or arm movements and inevitably needs to do full-body movements. If these obvious movements are necessary it is also more likely that passers-by notice the interaction process. We further observed that users tend to cover broader angles if they feel insecure with the provided feedback. Therefore, we argue that the covered angle span could give insights on how physical demanding and conspicuous an interaction technique is.

4.6   Limitations

One technical limitation is that out application used predefined angles to trigger the scanning mode in the *tactile only* and *combined* condition. This limited the user's interaction space in advance, but doesn't limit the potential set of measures itself. The automatic detection of scan events is another limitation, as this technique might come with inaccuracies, i.e., the detection of a scan event where is none. We further want to point out that the described study is by design not capable to give any insights on how effective the derived metrics are to actually distinguish between different scanning techniques. Finally, we want to emphasize that the vaguely illustrated potential impacts have been derived from mostly subjective impressions, i.e., the experimenter's observations and the participants' comments during the interview.

5   Conclusions

In this paper we identified an initial set of objective measures, i.e., frequency, duration, walking speed, angle span, with which a scan event can be technically defined independently of any concrete scenario. We argue that this set of measures potentially allows the systematic and objective analysis and comparison of scanning-based interaction techniques. We further illustrate the potential impact, e.g., increase of mental demand, each of the measures might have on a user.

It is important to understand and consider the set of measures as a mean to support and improve the overall design process. If a researcher or designer is going to design a new scanning-based interaction concept, the proposed set of measures can help to gain an understanding on what a scanning movement actually is and how the individual parameters might affect the user. Already existing interaction concepts could be analysed and thereby ideas for improvement can be revealed. If the research community starts to apply these measures, eventually some design guidelines for scanning-based interaction techniques might evolve.

We want to emphasize that the presented set of measures is a draft and the identified impact on the user have been derived from mostly subjective impressions. Obviously, future work is needed to establish the idea and validate the existing set. We plan to support the future efforts in this field by publishing our logging-based observation tool.

Acknowledgements. The authors are grateful to the European Commission, which co-funds the IP HaptiMap (FP7-ICT-224675). We like to thank our colleagues for sharing their ideas with us.

References

1. Barnard, L., Yi, J.S., Jacko, J.A., Sears, A.: An empirical comparison of use-in-motion evaluation scenarios for mobile computing devices. International Journal of Human-Computer Studies 62, 487–520 (2005)
2. Magnusson, C., Rassmus-Gröhn, K., Szymczak, D.: Scanning angles for directional pointing. In: Proceedings of MobileHCI (2010)
3. Magnusson, C., Rassmus-Gröhn, K., Szymczak, D.: The Influence of Angle Size in Navigation Applications Using Pointing Gestures. In: Nordahl, R., Serafin, S., Fontana, F., Brewster, S. (eds.) HAID 2010. LNCS, vol. 6306, pp. 107–116. Springer, Heidelberg (2010)
4. Oulasvirta, A., Tamminen, S., Roto, V., Kuorelahti, J.: Interaction in 4-second bursts: the fragmented nature of attentional resources in mobile hci. In: Proceedings of CHI (2005)
5. Pielot, M., Poppinga, B., Boll, S.: PocketNavigator: vibro-tactile waypoint navigation for everyday mobile devices. In: Proceedings of MobileHCI (2010)
6. Pielot, M., Poppinga, B., Heuten, W., Boll, S.: 6th Senses for Everyone! The Value of Multimodal Feedback in Handheld Navigation Aids. In: Proceedings of ICMI (2011)
7. Pielot, M., Poppinga, B., Heuten, W., Boll, S.: A Tactile Compass for Eyes-Free Pedestrian Navigation. In: Campos, P., Graham, N., Jorge, J., Nunes, N., Palanque, P., Winckler, M. (eds.) INTERACT 2011, Part II. LNCS, vol. 6947, pp. 640–656. Springer, Heidelberg (2011)
8. Rümelin, S., Rukzio, E., Hardy, R.: NaviRadar: A Novel Tactile Information Display for Pedestrian Navigation. In: Proceedings of UIST 2011 (2011)
9. Robinson, S.: Heads-up engagement with the real world: multimodal techniques for bridging the physical-digital divide. In: Proceedings of CHI (2010)
10. Robinson, S., Eslambolchilar, P., Jones, M.: Sweep-Shake: finding digital resources in physical environments. In: Proceedings of MobileHCI (2009)

Knocking Sound as Quality Sign
for Household Appliances and the Evaluation
of the Audio-Haptic Interaction

M. Ercan Altinsoy

Chair of Communication Acoustics, Dresden University of Technology, Germany
ercan.altinsoy@tu-dresden.de

Abstract. It has been known for a long time in the automobile industry that the first contact between the customer and a car in the showroom consists of opening the door, sitting in the car and closing the door. Therefore, the sounds of the door opening and closing are carefully designed to invoke feelings of high quality and safety in the customer. Of course, the vehicle's operating noises are equally crucial to the perception of overall quality.

The operating noises of household appliances have gained increasing importance because these noises can negatively or positively influence our daily life. When shopping, customers consider the sound power level of the household appliance provided by the manufacturers. In most cases, it is not possible to listen to the machine in operation. However, a common practice of customers is to knock the sidewalls or open and close the doors of the machine. The knocking sound carries information about the quality and solidity of the product and its material properties. The perception of the knocking sound is normally coupled to a tactile/kinesthetic impression of the knocking event. The aims of this study are to identify the perceptually important features of the knocking sound that affect the impression of quality, define the guidelines for a target sound, make suggestions regarding structural modifications to realize the target sound, and investigate the interaction between auditory and haptic stimuli in the overall product-quality assessment. To achieve these aims, experiments with unimodal and multimodal stimulus presentations were conducted. The results showed that an optimal knocking sound is dull, moderately loud, atonal, and has no distinctive long-lasting frequency components, particularly at high frequencies. A quality index was proposed based on psychoacoustic metrics. The physical coupling between the sound and the vibrations causes that both sensory cues have similar effects on perceived quality.

Keywords: Household appliances, vibration of plates, product sound quality, impulsive sounds, auditory-haptic interaction.

1 Introduction

Perception allows us to gather information regarding our environment using sensory inputs [1] and to identify events and objects in this environment. Therefore, each sound can be regarded as an information carrier that has a meaning to the listener [2].

C. Magnusson, D. Szymczak, and S. Brewster (Eds.): HAID 2012, LNCS 7468, pp. 121–130, 2012.
© Springer-Verlag Berlin Heidelberg 2012

Our perceptual system is very sensitive to impulsive or impact sounds, which are one of the most common sounds experienced in everyday life. In recent years, several studies have discussed identifying the material or size of an object using impact sounds [1, 3, and 4]. The results of these studies show that the signal frequency and duration are two important properties used to identify the sound sources that contribute to the impact event. The signal frequencies are used by humans primarily to estimate the geometrical properties of the sound sources [4]. Materials are identified from impact sounds primarily through damping and signal frequencies [1, 3]. If a listener hears a sound, she/he can identify different properties of the sound sources (e.g., material, location, or size), and she/he simultaneously interprets the perceived sound (auditory event) with regard to her/his expectations and living situation. As a result of this process, the listener can assign a quality value to the auditory event. The acoustic characteristics of sounds produced by consumer products are an integral part of product identity [2]. Therefore, there is a strong link between the sounds that are first heard by a customer visiting a dealership and the perceived image of a product, separate from the link between the product's operational sounds and its image. This link has been demonstrated in various studies using the sounds of opening and closing a car door and the resulting perceived quality of a vehicle [5, 6]. The results of these studies show that various sound properties that indicate the use of high-quality material (such as sealing and metal) play an important role in communicating an impression of quality to the customer. However, the overall pleasantness of the sound also plays an important role in the quality evaluation.

This study focuses on household appliances. According to marketing experts, customers will commonly knock the sides, press the buttons, and open and close the doors of a machine. The sounds, vibrations, and force-feedback that occur during these interactions provide the customer an impression of the product's quality. The objectives of this study are to investigate the relationship between the properties of the knocking sound and the perceived quality, define guidelines for the target sound, make suggestions regarding structural modifications to realize the target sound, and investigate the audio-haptic interaction of the knocking event. In the first experiment, a semantic differential investigation was conducted to evaluate the qualities of knocking sounds. In this experiment, recordings of the sound from knocking the sidewalls of 7 washing machines and filtered variations of the recordings were presented to the subjects. Then, a link between the perceptually important signal properties and the psychoacoustical metrics was established. In the next step, the subjects evaluated the quality of the appliance using only the haptic perception evoked by knocking the sidewall. Finally, an experiment with multimodal (auditory-haptic) stimuli was conducted. The remainder of the paper is organized as follows: the physical generation of the knocking sound is discussed in Section 2. The evaluation experiments of knocking sounds are described in Section 3. Finally, the evaluation experiments of haptic feedbacks and audio-haptic interaction are discussed in Section 4.

2   The Generation Mechanism of the Knocking Sound

The sidewalls of a household appliance (e.g., a washing machine or dish washer) can be considered clamped rectangular plates. The sound generated by knocking a sidewall depends on the bending wave characteristics of the plate (Figure 1). The Young's modulus and density of the material and the geometrical properties of the plate determine the speed of the bending wave [7]. According to [8], the first two eigenfrequencies of the plate are

$$f_1 = 1.57 \cdot \sqrt{\frac{E \cdot h^2}{12 \cdot (1 - \mu^2) \cdot \rho} \frac{1}{a^2}} \sqrt{5.14 + 3.13 \cdot \left(\frac{a}{b}\right)^2 + 5.14 \left(\frac{a}{b}\right)^4} \tag{1}$$

$$f_2 = 1.57 \cdot \sqrt{\frac{E \cdot h^2}{12 \cdot (1 - \mu^2) \cdot \rho} \frac{1}{a^2}} \sqrt{39.06 + 11.65 \cdot \left(\frac{a}{b}\right)^2 + 5.14 \left(\frac{a}{b}\right)^4} \tag{2}$$

where E is the Young's modulus of the sidewall material, h is the plate thickness, μ is Poisson's ratio, ρ is the material's density, a is the height of the sidewall and b is its length. The equations for the higher frequencies can be found in [7]. During knocking, several frequencies of the plate will be excited with various decay times. Figure 1 shows the typical time course and spectrogram of the sound pressure level of a knocking sound. Knocking generates an impulsive sound that contains a variety of frequency components. The following equation can be used to describe this sound:

$$x(t) = A_1 \cdot e^{-\delta_1 t} \cdot \sin \omega_1 + A_2 \cdot e^{-\delta_2 t} \cdot \sin \omega_2 + \cdots + A_n \cdot e^{-\delta_n t} \cdot \sin \omega_n \tag{3}$$

where A is the amplitude, δ is the damping constant, and ω is the angular frequency of each sinusoidal component. According to 1 and 2, the length, height, and thickness of the plate can determine the frequencies (ω) that are excited. The frequencies also depend on the Young's modulus and density of the sidewall material and any additional stiffness obtained through ribs. Any additional damping (e.g., a damping coating) can influence the decay time (δ). The applied force (or velocity) determines the amplitudes of the sinusoidal components, and the position of the knocking influences which modes are more or less strongly excited.

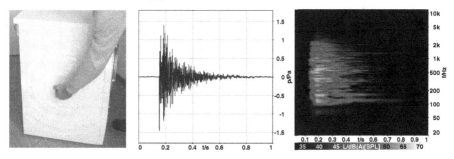

Fig. 1. Picture of a person by knocking the side wall of a washing machine, the time course of the sound pressure level and the spectrogram of an example knocking sound

3   Evaluation of Knocking Sounds

The goal of this experiment is to evaluate how different knocking sounds affect the perception of quality, to identify the perceptually important properties of the knocking sounds, and to define a target knocking sound for a high-quality washing machine.

3.1   Stimuli

Knocking sounds from the sidewalls of 7 different washing machines were recorded using a microphone (Brüel & Kjær, Type 2671). The recording setup is shown in Figure 2. A pendulum mechanism was used to ensure that the applied velocity and applied force remain constant during the recordings. A 50-gram mass, which has the typical impedance characteristics of a human hand, was installed on the end of a string. The experimenter grasped the mass, pulled it so that the string was inclined approximately 30 degrees from the vertical, and released it. The recordings were analyzed, and then additional sound stimuli were generated by filtering important frequency components (e.g. tonal components such as 120 Hz, 180 Hz, 1450 Hz, etc. in Figure 1c using band pass filters, high or low frequency ranges using high or low pass filters) or shortening the duration of the sound. The modified sounds are still perceived as usual knocking sounds. A total of 37 sound stimuli (7 original, 30 synthesized) were used in this study.

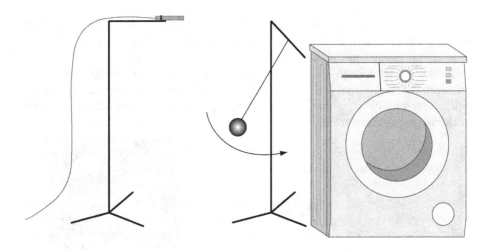

Fig. 2. Setup for recording knocking sounds

3.2   Subjects

Twenty-two subjects, twelve men and ten women aged between twenty-three and fifty-two years, participated in the experiment. The subjects had no specific knowledge regarding acoustics or vibrations. All of the subjects exhibited normal hearing (tested) and were paid for their participation on an hourly basis.

3.3   Experimental Setup and Procedure

All of the stimuli were presented using a loudspeaker (Genelec 8040 APM) located 1.15 m from the listener and visually masked using an acoustically transparent curtain. The presentation sound level was calibrated. The experiments were conducted in a sound-attenuating room.

In the training phase, all of the participants were presented with different combinations of stimuli from across the full stimulus range, and they were then familiarized with the procedure of the experiment. A semantic differential (SD) investigation of the perceived quality of the knocking sounds was conducted. The SD list consists of 12 attributes: overall quality, pleasant, solid, loud, high-frequency, muffled, hard, rickety, lingering, strong, tonal, expressive. A Matlab graphical user interface was used for the experiment. The subjects indicated the intensity of their associations on a continuous 100-point unnumbered graphical scale, which was marked with verbal anchors describing different intensities (not at all, slightly, moderately, very, extremely) [9].

3.4   Results

A factor analysis was conducted on the semantic differential data using a varimax rotation. This factor analysis revealed three combined factors that explained 79% of the variance (Table 1). The adjectives that exhibit loadings higher than 0.7 for a particular factor are listed among the factor's attributes. The first factor was termed high-quality and explains almost half of the variance. Correlations between the ratings of quality and the attributes of the signal are presented in Table 2. The results reveal a strong correlation between the quality ratings and the high-frequency and muffled attributes of the sound. The knocking sounds that contain primarily low-frequency components were judged to indicate higher quality than the knocking sounds containing primarily high-frequency components. Other terms interact with each other and contribute to the perceived quality. Quiet and sharp sounds evoked better quality ratings than loud and sharp sounds. Particularly high levels of each attribute result in a low perceived quality. If a sound is too loud or too quiet, it receives a low quality rating.

Table 1. Factor analysis results for the knocking sounds

Factors	Attributes	% Variance
Factor 1: High quality	Quality, loud, high(frequency), tonal, muffled, lingering, rickety, strong, expressive	39
Factor 2: Pleasantness	Pleasant, loud, high(frequency), tonal	21
Factor 3: Solidity	Solid, loud, high(frequency), muffled, lingering, hard, rickety, strong	19

The second factor was termed pleasantness, and the third was called solidity. The relationship between these factors and the attributes of the sound exhibit some similarities to the relationship between the quality ratings and the sound attributes. Most of the signal-related attributes, including high-frequency, loudness, and muffled play a role in each of the three combined factors: high quality, pleasantness, and solidity. It is obvious that the tonality does not play a role on the solidity rating. The results reveal that a target high-quality knocking sound should have as little high-frequency content as possible, no distinctive time structure (no lingering), little tonality and a moderate volume. In other words, the characteristics sharpness, lingering, and tonality are all strongly and negatively related to a perception of high quality.

A possible modification that could improve the perceived quality of the knocking sound is to coat the sidewalls with a vibration-damping material (see Equation 3). Such materials damp bending vibrations, particularly at high frequencies [10].

Table 2. Pearson correlation coefficients between the ratings of quality, pleasantness, and solidity and the ratings of the signal-related attributes

	quality	pleasant	solid
Loud	0.52	0.64	0.61
high(frequency)	0.81	0.83	0.81
muffled vs. lingering	0.72	0.70	0.82
Tonal	0.51	0.53	0.15

To develop a quality index for knocking sounds, the following psychoacoustic metrics of the stimuli were calculated:

- Sharpness (5 percentile), S_5, according to von Bismarck [11],
- Loudness, N, according to DIN 45631/A1[12],
- Tonality, T, according to Aures [13],

The previously described relationships between the perceived quality and the perceived signal-related attributes were used to choose the psychoacoustical metrics to evaluate. Aside from the attributes high-frequency, loud, and tonal, the perceived muffled quality of the sound (vs. lingering) is an important signal-related attribute that affects the perceived quality. In Figure 4, short-time Fourier transform (STFT)-based spectrograms of three knocking sounds containing different long-lasting frequency components are shown. The decay times and frequencies of the individual frequency components can be used to model the perceived level of the muffled attribute. Therefore, each frequency band of the stimulus was separated using a bandpass Chebyshev Filter and analyzed using a level vs. time analysis, and the audible duration (from the beginning of the sound to silence) was calculated. The sounds containing high-frequency components with long decay times (for example, Figure 4a) received lower quality ratings than the sounds containing low-frequency components with long decay times (for example, Figures 4b and c). Therefore, the audible decay time results were weighted using the sharpness results of the knocking sounds. The weightings of the psychoacoustical metrics, which were given in Figure 3, were determined considering the relationship between the quality ratings of the knocking sounds and the results of the psychoacoustical metrics. Additional criterion was the differences in the numerical values of the metrics. The Pearson correlation coefficient between the quality index based on the psychoacoustical metrics and the obtained quality ratings was 0.89.

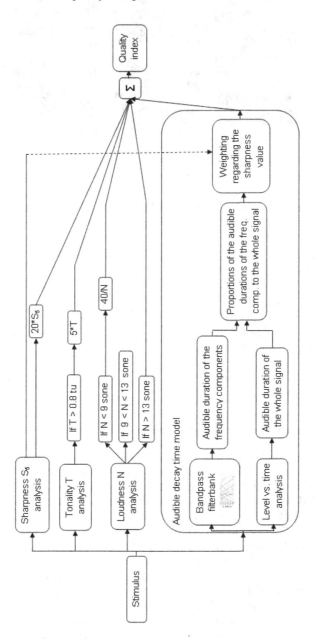

Fig. 3. The knocking sound quality index model

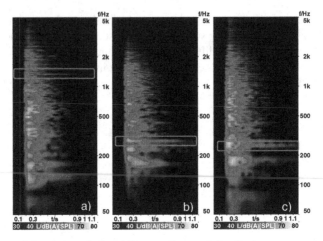

Fig. 4. Spectrogram of three example knocking sounds containing frequency components with long decay times

4 Evaluation of Audio-Haptic Interaction Regarding Knocking Event

If a customer knocks the sidewall of a washing machine, she/he not only hears the knocking sound, but she/he also perceives the force-feedback and the vibrations of the side wall. It is important to determine whether the quality evaluation considers an interaction between auditory and haptic feedback. If two modalities are combined, the resulting multimodal percept may be a weaker, stronger, or altogether different percept, and it is also possible for one modality to dominate an overall assessment [14]. Therefore, two experiments were conducted to investigate the issue of haptic-auditory interaction. In the first experiment, the subjects evaluated quality using only haptic feedback, and in the second experiment, the subjects evaluated the quality using both haptic and auditory feedback.

4.1 Haptic Quality Evaluation Experiment

Twenty subjects, ten men and ten women aged between 21 and 54 years, participated in the experiment. None of these subjects participated in the previous investigation. The subjects had no specific knowledge of vibration or acoustics. All of the subjects were right-handed. The subjects knocked the sidewalls of 7 different *original* washing machines and evaluated their quality. To prevent the subjects from obtaining visual information, they wore eye patches. To mask the knocking sound, the subjects wore closed dynamic headphones (Sennheiser HDA 200) with sound isolation levels of 15 dB at 125 Hz and 29 dB at 1 kHz. In addition to this passive attenuation, pink noise was supplied at 80 dB(A). In the training, subjects were instructed to knock the walls with a constant velocity of 1.0 m/s, which was controlled visually by the experimenter during the experiment. Each subject was presented the stimuli in a different order. The subjects indicated the intensity of their associations on the same scale as in the previous investigation. The results of the experiment are presented in Section 4.3.

4.2   Audio-Haptic Quality Evaluation Experiment

Twenty-two subjects, thirteen men and nine women aged between 24 and 50 years, participated in this experiment. None of these subjects participated in the previous investigations. The task of the subjects in this experiment was to knock the sidewalls of 7 different original washing machines and evaluate the quality of the machine using auditory and haptic feedback. Visual information was masked using eye patches. All of the other aspects of the experiment, such as training, stimuli-order, and the procedure were the same as in the previous investigation. The results of the experiment are presented in Section 4.3.

4.3   Results of the haptic and the Audio-Haptic Quality Evaluation Experiments

The quality judgments in the audio-only, haptic-only and audio-haptic experiments were averaged, and the mean scores are shown in Figure 5. In haptic quality evaluation experiments, it was observed that high rigidity and no long-lasting vibrations evoke the impression of high quality. The standard deviations vary from 16 to 22 under the different stimulus conditions. Except for the results of Stimulus 5, the effects of receiving different stimuli are insignificant. However, some tendencies are apparent. No modality is observed to dominate the overall quality judgments. The relationships among the modalities are dependent on the stimuli on which the judgment is based. The results show that the auditory-haptic quality ratings are not always the same as the unimodal (auditory or haptic) quality ratings. The audio and haptic quality ratings differ from each other strongly in the case of Stimulus 5. In this case, the low haptic quality rating causes a low quality rating in the multimodal experiment, though the knocking sound was perceived to indicate high quality. In Stimulus 3, the two individual modalities interact and lead to a combined perceptual event. However, in some cases (Stimulus 2), the haptic perception is the dominant modality. In almost half of the cases (for example Stimuli 4, 6, and 7), the knocking sound and haptic feedback were obtained very similar quality ratings. One reason is that the knocking sound is produced by the side wall vibrations and therefore both stimuli carry similar information and achieve similar quality ratings.

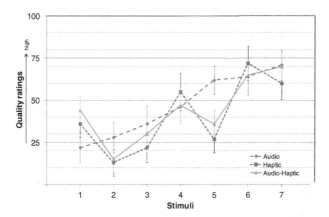

Fig. 5. The quality judgments under audio-only, haptic-only and audio-haptic conditions

5   Conclusions

In this study, the perceptually important features of knocking sounds were investigated in terms of the perceived quality of the washing machines generating the sounds. The results reveal that particularly sharp and lingering (long-duration) sounds were judged as signs of bad quality. An optimal knocking sound that indicates the high quality is dull, moderately loud, atonal, and has no distinctive long-lasting frequency components, particularly at high frequencies. An index based on psychoacoustic metrics including the sharpness according to von Bismarck, the tonality according to Aures, the loudness according to DIN 45631, and a weighted decay time model, was developed to predict the perceived quality of the knocking sound. An optimal haptic feedback that indicates the high quality has features such as high rigidity and no long-lasting vibrations. Therefore the coating the sidewalls with a vibration-damping material can improve the perceived quality of knocking sound and haptic feedback. Audio-haptic quality evaluation experiments demonstrated that it is not possible to say that there is a dominant modality in multimodal quality perception.

References

1. Giordano, B.L.: Sound Source Perception in Impact Sounds. Ph.D. Thesis. University of Padova, Italy (2005)
2. Jekosch, U.: Meaning in the Context of Sound Quality Assessment. Acta Acustica 85, 681–684 (1999)
3. Klatzky, R.L., Pai, D.K., Krotkov, E.P.: Perception of Material from Contact Sounds. Presence: Teleoperators and Virtual Environment 9(4), 399–410 (2000)
4. Lakatos, S., McAdams, S., Caussé, R.: The Representation of Auditory Source Characteristics: Simple Geometric Form. Perception & Psychophysics 59(8), 1180–1190 (1997)
5. Parizet, E., Guyader, E., Nosulenko, V.: Analysis of Car Door Closing Sound Quality. Applied Acoustics 69, 12–22 (2008)
6. Liebing, R.: Subjektive Bewertung von instationären Funktionsgeräuschen. Ph.D. Thesis, Oldenburg University (2009)
7. Henn, H., Sinambari, G.R., Fallen, M.: Ingenieurakustik. Vieweg, Wiesbaden (2001)
8. Leissa, A.W.: Vibration of Plates. NASA SP-160, Washington D.C. (1969)
9. Altinsoy, M.E., Jekosch, U.: The Semantic Space of Vehicle Sounds: Developing a Semantic Differential with Regard to Customer Perception. Journal of Audio Engineering Society 60(1/2), 13–20 (2012)
10. Tarnoczy, T.: Vibration of metal plates covered with vibration damping layers. Journal of Sound and Vibration 11, 299–307 (1970)
11. Von Bismarck, G.: Timbre of steady sounds: a factorial investigation of its verbal attributes. Acustica 30, 146–158 (1974)
12. DIN 45631/A1: Calculation of loudness level and loudness from the sound spectrum - Zwicker method – Amend. 1: Calculation of the loudness of time-variant sound (2008)
13. Aures, W.: Berechnungsverfahren für den sensorischen Wohlklang beliebiger Schallsignale. Acustica 59, 130–141 (1985)
14. Altinsoy, M.E.: Auditory-Tactile Interaction in Virtual Environments. Shaker Verlag, Germany (2006)

Spectral Discrimination Thresholds Comparing Audio and Haptics for Complex Stimuli

Lorenzo Picinali[1], Christopher Feakes[1], Davide A. Mauro[2], and Brian F.G. Katz[3]

[1] De Montfort University, The Gateway, LE1 9BJ Leicester, UK
[2] LIM-Dipartimento di Informatica, via Comelico 39/41, 20135 Milano, Italia
[3] LIMSI-CNRS, Université Paris-Sud, 91403 Orsay, France

Abstract. Individuals with normal hearing are generally able to discriminate auditory stimuli that have the same fundamental frequency but different spectral content. This study concerns to what extent it is possible to perform the same differentiation considering vibratory tactile stimuli. Three perceptual experiments have been carried out in an attempt to compare discrimination thresholds in terms of spectral differences between auditory and vibratory tactile stimulations. The first test consists of assessing the subject's ability in discriminating between three signals with distinct spectral content. The second test focuses on the measurement of the discrimination threshold between a pure tone signal and a signal composed of two pure tones, varying the amplitude and frequency of the second tone. Finally, in the third test the discrimination threshold is measured between a tone with even harmonic components and a tone with odd ones. The results show that it is indeed possible to discriminate between haptic signals having the same fundamental frequency but different spectral. The threshold of sensitivity for detection is markedly less than for audio stimuli.

1 Introduction

Humans are readily able to distinguish between the aural timbre of common notes played by different instruments (for example between an A3 played on a clarinet and the same note played on a flute). The current study investigates whether or not it is possible to observe a similar ability in terms of vibratory tactile sensations.

Vibratory tactile stimulations are often employed to assist in the creation of virtual objects in a computer simulation, or again to support and facilitate specific tasks within a multimodal interactive application. Haptic vibratory actuators can be found in mobile phones, tablet PCs, etc. and are used to enhance the interactivity of the device, and to transfer selected information to the user (e.g. the arrival of an incoming phone call). Typically the types of information transferred through vibration have been of a *boolean* nature, employing single or a series of *on* or *off* signals (e.g. simple alert for an incoming call). With improvements in tractor response and performance, amplitude and frequency modulation of the vibratory stimulus have started to be used in the form of tactons (see Brown, 2006) and, more in general, of vibratory patterns. Nevertheless, variations in the spectral characteristics of the vibratory signal are rarely employed. It is generally assumed that the human sensitivity to such differences, regarding vibratory tactile stimulation, is not particularly high.

C. Magnusson, D. Szymczak, and S. Brewster (Eds.): HAID 2012, LNCS 7468, pp. 131–140, 2012.
© Springer-Verlag Berlin Heidelberg 2012

While studies investigating the ability of the human tactile system to discriminate between signals with different frequency have been successfully carried out in the past (see Verrillo, 1963 and Verrillo et al., 1992), similar investigations on the discrimination between signals with different spectral characteristics have only recently started to be performed (see Merchel et al., 2010).

The hypothesis at the base of this study is that the human tactile system can indeed discriminate between vibrations with the same fundamental frequency but different spectral characteristics. The objective is therefore to investigate how spectral variations are perceived through tactile vibratory stimulation, and to compare these results with those measured for auditory stimulations.

2   Related Works

It is well known that differences in the frequency content and spectral envelope of acoustic signals are often perceived as timbre variations, allowing for the differentiation between stimuli with the same fundamental frequency, loudness and duration, while having different spectral characteristics (an overview on studies in this field can be found in Moore, 2003, pp. 105-107 and pp. 270-273). But, is it possible to similarly differentiate complex vibratory tactile stimuli?

Previous studies have investigated the perceptual aspects of frequency and amplitude variations in tactile vibratory stimulations. In Verrillo, 1963, the subjective perceived intensity as a function of the vibration frequency has been studied and compared in relation to the contact area. Results showed that for pure tones detection thresholds improved with frequency, from 25 Hz to 200-300 Hz, at a rate of about 12 dB/octave, then decreasing with the same slope to about 1000 Hz. The larger the contact area (up to 5.1 cm^2), the lower the threshold.

In Verrillo et al., 1992, various studies are reported on frequency and amplitude discrimination for tactile stimuli using pure tones, pulses, and narrow-band noise signals. Comparing the frequency discrimination thresholds between audio and tactile modalities highlights that while the ear can discriminate frequency differences of the order of 0.3%, the performances of the skin were found to be much lower, of the order of 30%. In terms of amplitude discrimination, the threshold for vibratory stimulation was found to be between 0.4 and 2.3 dB, values that are very similar to the threshold for auditory stimulation (between 0.5 and 1 dB, as reported in Moore, 2003, pp. 139-139). Furthermore, the tactile system was found to be capable of processing vibrations within a dynamic range of 55 dB, compared to a sensibly larger range for the auditory system (120 dB, see Moore, 2003, pp. 127-128).

In West and Cutkosky, 1997, the possibility of using a haptic device for displaying fine surface features was investigated. Comparative tests were conducted using both a stylus and fingertips, outlining how the perception of sinusoidal features was qualitatively similar when comparing real and virtual walls. A similar study has been presented in Choi and Tan, 2005, where more sophisticated haptic rendering algorithms were used for rendering complex surface textures of different virtual objects.

In Branje, 2010 a sensory substitution system, aimed at translating music into vibrations presented on the human back, was evaluated in a frequency discrimination task.

Findings outlined that vibrotactile stimulation can indeed be used for supporting the experience of music even in absence of sound. Furthermore, voice coils were found to be suitable for transmitting certain sound characteristics in the form of tactile vibrations.

The ability to discriminate between different signals and design parameters for the generation of tactile feedback has been investigated in Merchel et al., 2010. In this study, experiments were conducted in an attempt to determine whether one can distinguish different looped audio signals rendered through an electro-dynamic shaker positioned under a touch-sensitive screen. Stimuli differed in their spectral content and rhythmic characteristics. Results outlined that a distinction was indeed possible. Additional studies have examined the advantage of audio, tactile and coupled audio-haptic stimuli (Altinsoy and Merchel, 2009), although there was no direct relation between the audio and tactile stimuli selected.

Basic studies performed using pure and/or very simple tones for quantifying the discrimination thresholds in terms of spectral variations for tactile stimuli have not been found in literature. The use of an experimental protocol which employs the same stimuli design for both audio and haptic modalities is seen as a fundamental study which is currently absent. The current study proposes an evaluation of the discrimination ability and sensitivity to complex haptic stimuli as compared to auditory stimuli as a reference using a common protocol.

3 Preliminary Study Using Audio-haptic Source Differentiation

A recent study by the authors concerned the exploitation of audio and/or haptic cues for the selection of a desired target in a 3D virtual environment containing multiple distractors (see Menelas et al., 2010). In order to promote coherent identification of audio-haptic targets, four haptic signatures were designed using waveform amplitude modulation. These signatures were defined empirically in order to obtain a clear distinction during the actual targeting task. The equations used for generating the different vibratory stimuli were the following:

$$
\begin{aligned}
W_1 &= a\sin(2\pi \times 121dt) & W_3 &= a\sin(2\pi \times 3dt)\sin(2\pi \times 121dt) \\
W_2 &= a\sin(2\pi \times 0.5dt)\sin(2\pi \times 121dt) & W_4 &= a\sin(2\pi \times 31dt)\sin(2\pi \times 53dt)
\end{aligned}
\tag{1}
$$

W_1 defines a sinusoidal vibration at 121 Hz. W_2 is an amplitude modulation of W_1 by a 0.5 Hz sinusoid, producing the sensation of a rhythmic pulsing vibration. W_3 is a modulation of W_1 by a 3 Hz sinusoid, producing the sensation of rapid impulse vibration. W_4 is a 53 Hz sinusoid modulated by a 31 Hz whose combination resulted in a rather rough vibration sensation due to the inharmonicity of the two components.

The availability of spectral discrimination thresholds for vibratory stimuli (aim of the current study) would have allowed a more direct, parametric, and precise stimuli definition process, facilitating creation of multiple distinguishable haptic signatures.

4 Experimental Study

Aiming at investigating the differences between audio vibratory tactile perceptions relative to the detection of spectral variations between signals with the same fundamental frequency, three tests have been designed and carried out.

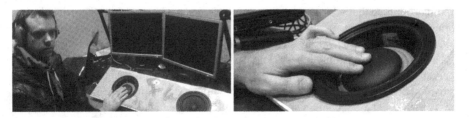

Fig. 1. (left) Haptic test stimuli protocol, including the use of noise-suppression headphones. (left driver) Cone removed and added dome for haptic stimuli, (right drive) unmodified for audio stimuli. (right) Hand of a participant, showing the wrist resting on the wooden board and the three mid-fingers placed on the plastic dome.

The order and complexity of the tests is related to the two aims of the study: (1) to identify any difference between the two modalities, and (2) to quantify this difference. In the first test, the ability to discriminate between three signals with different spectral characteristics is assessed for the auditory and haptic modalities. This is a relatively trivial auditory task, and the audio component is included just as a reference. The second and third tests aim at quantifying the discrimination thresholds between signals with the same fundamental frequency but different spectral content; tone/2-tones discrimination, odd and even harmonics components discrimination. The use of the same hardware and software for the delivery of the auditory and haptic feedback was made in order to facilitate a consistent comparison of results between the two modalities.

Participants consisted of 12 subjects, 8 males/4 females, aged 19 – 52 years. Each test session took approximately one hr: 5 min for the calibration, 15 min for the first test, 30 min for the second test, and 10 min for the third.

4.1   Experimental Apparatus

The experimental apparatus is composed of a software component, a computer, an audio interface, an audio amplifier and two 8 inch loudspeaker woofer drivers, mounted on a wooden board (see Fig. 1): one of these has been modified by removing the speaker cone. A coupling system (a rigid 10 cm diameter plastic dome, on which the fingers of the subjects are placed) was installed in order to transfer the vibrations of the coil to the hand. The subjects are instructed to rest their dominant hand on the wooden board surrounding the driver, and to position the last phalanx of their middle three fingers (index, middle, and ring fingers) on the plastic dome, without applying any pressure (see Fig. 1). These choices (hand position, parts of the finger to be in contact with the vibratory actuator, etc.) have been made based on Verrillo, 1962 and Verrillo, 1963. Considering the audio rendering modality, the subjects have been asked to place their head at 1 m from the driver. All subjects completed tests for both modalities. The generation and processing of the signals, the testing procedures and the data collection have all been implemented in a Max/MSP [1] platform/patch. The digital signals are sent to a MOTU Traveler FireWire audio interface, converted to analogue signals, and sent to

----
[1] http://www.cycling74.com

an Oniphonics Footprint 150 amplifier, and then to one of the two drivers, depending on the testing modality. Frequencies could be generated between 35 Hz and 1400 Hz without any notable resonance outside the dynamic range of ± 10 dB (un-weighted).

4.2 Calibration

After a series of informal trials and evaluations, and reviewing previous literature in the field of auditory and vibratory-tactile perception (see Sec. 2) as well as the limitations of the playback system, the frequency ranges for the tests have been set at 35-250 Hz for haptic, and 200-1400 Hz for audio.

The audio modality signal amplification has been calibrated in order to generate a SPL value of 70 dB A-weighted for a 1000 Hz pure tone at 1 m distance from the loudspeaker driver (head location during audio tests). This value has been chosen considering the standard levels used in audiological evaluations (Penrod, 1985).

Due to the sensitivity of thresholds to contact area, the haptic feedback level calibration stage is performed for each subject individually. The participants are asked to place their fingers on the plastic dome (see Sec. 4.1) while a 100 Hz sinusoidal stimulus is reproduced. The level is increased until the subjects can just perceive a vibration. The signal gain is then increased by 20 dB, in order to have a clear presentation level and to assure consistency in the haptic presentation stimuli across subjects. The rendered level is therefore calibrated at *Threshold of Perceptibility (100 Hz)+20 dB*.

During haptic testing, the SPL produced by the cone-less driver was between 50 dB and 57 dB A-weighted (measured at 100 Hz), depending on the level calibration described in the previous paragraph, while the background noise in the testing environment was 32 dB A-weighted. In order to avoid auditory stimulation from the haptic driver, a pair of passive noise-suppression headphones were used (see Fig. 1) which provided a sound level reduction of 20 dB (manufacture's statement). No subject reported hearing the audio signal produced by the haptic device during the test.

4.3 Test One: Signal Comparison

The subjects were asked to discriminate between three types of simple signals:

(a) *Single pure tone* (Sine): frequency chosen in the middle of the ranges for the two modalities, therefore $f_1^h = 100$ Hz for haptic and $f_1^a = 600$ Hz for audio.
(b) *Narrow-band noise* (Noise): white noise processed with a band-pass filter centred at f_1^h for the haptic stimulus and at f_1^a for the audio stimulus.
(c) *Two concurrent pure tones* (2Sine): the first with frequency f_1^h or f_1^a for the two modalities, and the second with frequency $f_2 = f_1 \times 1.7$. This value has been chosen in order to generate an overtone with no harmonic relation to the fundamental.

The test consists of three separate trials for each rendering modality. For the first trial signals *a* and *b* are compared: 20 repetitions of two randomly selected signals (*a&b*, *b&a*, *a&a*, or *b&b*) are presented to the participant, who is asked to state, after each repetition, if the two signals are the same or if they are different. For the second trial, signals *b* and *c* are compared, for the third trial signals *a* and *c*. The two signals are reproduced in the following sequence: first signal for 1000 ms, 200 ms of silence, second

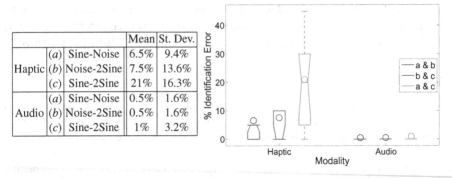

Fig. 2. (left) Mean and std of identification errors for test one. (right) Distribution of identification error for test one; — median, ○ mean. Values are displayed according to rendering modality and signal pairs for stimuli *a*: Sine, *b*: Noise, *c*: 2Sine.

signal for 1000 ms, with each signal processed with a 5 ms fade in and fade out. All signals are calibrated in order to generate the same dB RMS levels.

The percentage of identification errors in the discrimination task between the different pairs of signals are reported in Fig. 2. As expected, the audio modality error rate is quite low (mean of 0.7% over the three pairs, std 2.1), while for the haptic modality error rates are higher (mean of 11.7%, std 13.1). Furthermore, it can be noted that for the haptic modality the error rates for the first two trials are similar, while the third (Sine-2Sine) are notably higher. A similar relative increase is noted in the results for the audio modality. This can be justified considering that in the first two trials a periodic signal (*a* or *c*) is compared with a narrow-band noise (*b*), while in the third trial two sinusoidal signals are compared (*a* and *c*), making the discrimination task more complex.

The initial outcome of this test is that it is indeed possible to discriminate through the tactile sense between vibrations with equal (or similar) fundamental frequency and different spectral content.

4.4   Test Two: Two Tones Detection

Using a simple up-down 1 dB step adaptive procedure (Levitt, 1978), the discrimination threshold is measured between a pure tone signal and a stimulus composed of two concurrent pure tones, changing the amplitude and frequency of the second tone.

The participants are presented with groups of two stimuli in the following sequence: first signal for 1000 ms, 200 ms of silence, second signal for 1000 ms, with each signal processed with a 5 ms fade in and fade out. Initially, the two stimuli are the same (a pure tone *a* with frequency f_a). The second stimulus is then iteratively modified by adding to *a* another pure tone *b* with frequency f_b, increasing adaptively the amplitude of *b* and decreasing the one *a*, in order to maintain the same RMS level for both signals. The participants are then asked to determine when a difference can be heard between the first and the second stimulus. The test is then carried out adaptively until a threshold value is found (after 5 up-down direction changes).

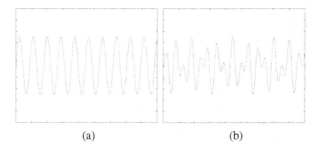

(a)   (b)

Fig. 3. (a) Waveform of the pure tone audio signal used for test two. (b) Waveform of the two-tones audio signal ($f_2 = f_1 \times 1.7$) used for test two. For the haptic rendering, the same signals have been used, with $f_a^h = 100$ Hz instead of $f_a^a = 500$ Hz.

The values of f_1 are set at 500 Hz for the audio modality, and 100 Hz for haptic. Six values have been chosen for the signal b, where f_b is a multiple of f_a defined by the multiplier factor m (for both modalities): $m = 0.5, 0.7, 1.7, 2.0, 2.7, 3.0$. These values are chosen in order to allow various combinations of two concurrent tones at different frequencies, with and without harmonic relations. Example waveforms of both signals are displayed in Fig. 3.

The discrimination threshold values, expressed in terms of dB difference between the a and b components in the second signal, are reported for each modality and for each value of m in Fig. 4.

There is a notable difference between the mean discrimination threshold values for the haptic modality (mean of -17.7 dB, std 8.3) and for audio (mean of -46.4 dB, std 11.9), the latter being distinctly lower (higher sensitivity). This quantifies the fact that the human hearing system is more sensitive in discriminating between a pure tone and a complex tone composed of two pure tones if compared with the tactile system.

Furthermore, it can be observed that for the haptic modality the values are generally lower (better performance) when f_2 is not in harmonic relation with f_1. For $m = 0.7, 1.7, 2.7$, the mean discrimination threshold is -20.2 dB (std 8.1), while for $m = 0.5, 2.0, 3.0$ it is -15.2 dB (std 9.4), a difference of 5.0 dB. A similar tendency can be observed for the audio modality, but in this case the difference is only of 2.3 dB.

Inferential statistics have been performed to identify whether the differences between groups are statistically significant. As the data sets are small and not normally distributed, exact Mann-Whitney tests were used. For the tactile stimulation, results with the in-harmonic f_2 components differ significantly from the harmonic ones (MW U = 431, p = 0.015), while for the auditory stimulation the differences between the two groups are not significant (MW U =569, p = 0.374). The effect size can be considered very small for both modalities, with $r = -0.706$ for tactile and $r = -0.26$ for audio.

An explanation could be attempted considering the fact that non-harmonic overtones are more likely to generate amplitude beats with the fundamental component, and these could be used to discriminate between different stimuli, offering a further cue for this experimental task. Nevertheless, this cue should be available for both modalities, and not only for the tactile one as outlined by the results of the Mann-Whitney test. At the moment, there does not seem to be a precise and clear explanation of this result.

	Haptic		Audio	
m	Mean	St. Dev.	Mean	St. Dev.
0.5	−20.9	9.3	−46.1	11.8
0.7	−21.6	7.8	−48.2	10.5
1.7	−19.3	7.8	−40.9	13.9
2.0	−13.6	5.6	−40.4	15.4
2.7	−19.8	9.1	−53.4	11.0
3.0	−11.2	10.3	−49.3	8.7

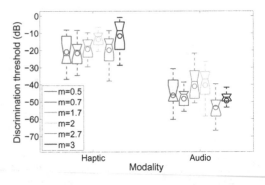

Fig. 4. (left) Mean and std of the discrimination threshold results for test two. (right) Distribution of discrimination threshold results for test two; — median, ○ mean. Values are displayed according to rendering modality and f_2 multiplier m.

Other tendencies can also be observed (e.g. the audio modality seems to be more sensitive to m,), though not enough data has yet been collected for allowing further statistical analysis (see Sec. 5).

4.5   Test Three: Spectral Detection

Using a simple up-down adaptive procedure (see Levitt, 1978), the discrimination threshold is measured between a tone with even harmonic components (such as the *typical* organ pipe) and a tone with odd harmonic components (such as the sound of the clarinet). The testing procedure is the same as for test two (see Sec. 4.4).

Initially, participants are presented with the same stimulus repeated twice (a pure tone with the first 3 even harmonic components, 2nd, 4th, and 6th, each one with an amplitude 3 dB lower than the previous). The second repetition is then changed adaptively, reducing the amplitude of the even harmonic components and increasing that of three odd harmonic components (3rd, 5th, and 7th). In order to maintain the same overall levels for both repetitions, the reduction and amplification of the harmonic components is performed using a cosine function on a 128-step linear scale from 0 to $\pi/2$ for the even harmonic components, and from $\pi/2$ to 0 for the odd ones. In Fig. 5 the waveform and spectrum of both signals are displayed.

The participants are asked to identify when a difference can be heard between the two stimuli. The test is carried out adaptively until a threshold value is found (after 5 up-down direction changes). The values of the fundamental frequency for the complex tone have been set at 200 Hz for the audio modality, and 35 Hz for the tactile one.

The discrimination threshold values, expressed as dB difference between the even-harmonics and odd-harmonics stimuli, are reported for each modality in Fig. 6. It is possible to observe that there is a sensible difference between the mean values for the haptic modality (mean of −15.3 dB, std 13.2) and for the audio one (mean of −27.7 dB, std 9.2). For the audio modality, it is therefore possible to discriminate between a tone with just even harmonic components and a tone with also odd harmonic components when the level difference between these is 27.7 dB, while this value decreases to 15.3 dB for the tactile rendering, a difference of 12.4 dB in harmonic detection sensitivity.

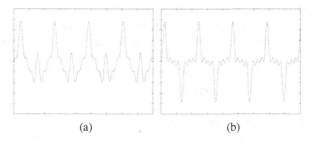

(a)   (b)

Fig. 5. (a) Waveform of the even-harmonic audio signal used for test three. (b) Waveform of the odd-harmonic audio signal used for test three. For the haptic rendering, the same signals have been used, but with a fundamental frequency of 35 Hz instead of 200 Hz, and the harmonics consequently scaled.

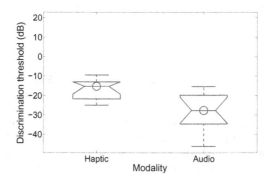

Fig. 6. Distribution of discrimination threshold results for test three by rendering modality; — median, ○ mean. Values are expressed as the difference in dB between the even-harmonics and odd-harmonics stimuli.

5   Conclusion

The initial outcomes of this series of perceptual evaluations comparing audio and haptic-vibratory senses is that for both modalities spectral differences between different stimuli with the same fundamental frequency can be perceived, with auditory perception being more sensitive when compared to tactile one.

In terms of discrimination thresholds between a pure tone and a stimulus composed of two pure tones, the difference between the two modalities was 28.7 dB, with haptic sensitivity being distinctly lower. Furthermore, a lower discrimination threshold (5 dB) for the haptic modality is found when the two tones composing the second stimulus are not in harmonic relation. A similar tendency, but with reduced magnitude, is also observed for the audio modality, but cannot be considered statistically significant for the current results. In terms of discrimination threshold between a tone with even harmonic components and a tone with odd harmonic components, the audio modality exhibited a sensitivity 12.4 dB greater than the haptic modality.

Considering the results reported in Merchel et al., 2010, where it was shown how haptic stimuli with different spectral and rhythmic characteristics could be discriminated, the results from the current study expand those outcomes outlining that discrimination is possible even between stimuli with no rhythmic features at all, and with solely spectral differences. Furthermore, referring to the preliminary study described in Sec. 3, the initial results of the current study could be employed for allowing the creation of a larger number of distinguishable tactile-vibratory signals. Considering for example the outcomes of test three, six distinguishable haptic signatures could be created changing the levels of the overtones between a signal with only even harmonic components and a signal with only odd ones. Moreover, the use of in-harmonic overtones could be exploited even further for allowing a higher discrimination factor.

This preliminary study is currently being repeated with a larger test population. Furthermore, these subsequent tests will be carried out on additional groups of visually and hearing impaired subjects, in an attempt to consider the case of individuals with and without sensory deprivations.

References

Altinsoy, M.E., Merchel, S.: Audiotactile Feedback Design for Touch Screens. In: Altinsoy, M.E., Jekosch, U., Brewster, S. (eds.) HAID 2009. LNCS, vol. 5763, pp. 136–144. Springer, Heidelberg (2009)

Branje, C., Maksimouski, M., Karam, M., Fels, D.I., Russo, F.: Vibrotactile Display of Music on the Human Back. In: ACHI 2010: International Conference on Advances in Computer-Human Interactions, St. Maarten, Netherlands, pp. 154–159 (2010)

Brown, L.M., Kaaresoja, T.: Feel who's talking: using tactons for mobile phone alerts. In: CHI 2006 Extended Abstracts on Human Factors in Computing Systems, Montreal, Canada, pp. 604–609 (2006)

Choi, S., Tan, H.Z.: Toward realistic haptic rendering of surface textures. IEEE Computer Graphics and Applications 24(2), 40–47 (2005)

Levitt, H.: Adaptive testing in audiology. Scand. Audiol. Suppl. 6, 241–291 (1978)

Menelas, B., Picinali, L., Bourdot, P., Katz, B.F.G.: Audio Haptic Feedbacks for an Acquisition Task in a Multi-Target Context. In: IEEE 3DUI User Interfaces Conf., Waltham, MA, US (2009)

Merchel, S., Altinsoy, E., Stamm, M.: Tactile Music Instrument Recognition for Audio Mixers. In: 128th Conv. of the Audio Egineering Society, London, UK (2010)

Moore, C.J.B.: An Introduction to the Psychology of Hearing. Academic Press, London (2003)

Penrod, J.I.: Speech Discrimination Testing. In: Katz, J. (ed.) Handbook of Clinical Audiology, Baltimore, MD, pp. 235–255

Verrillo, R.T.: Investigation of Some Parameters of the Cutaneous Threshold for Vibration. J. Acoust. Soc. Am. 34(11), 1768–1773 (1962)

Verrillo, R.T.: Effect of Contactor Area on the Vibrotactile Threshold. J. Acoust. Soc. Am. 37, 843–846 (1963)

Verrillo, R.T., Gescheider, G.A.: Perception via the Sense of Touch. Tactile Aids for the Hearing Impaired (1992); edited by Summers, I.R.: Whurr Publishers, London

West, A.M., Cutkosky, M.R.: Detection of Real and Virtual Fine Surface Features with a Haptic Interface and Stylus. In: 6th Annual Symposium on Haptic Interfaces, Dallas, TX (1997)

How Does Representation Modality Affect User-Experience of Data Artifacts?

Trevor Hogan and Eva Hornecker

Dept. of Computer and Information Sciences,
University of Strathclyde, Glasgow G11XH, UK
{trevor.hogan,eva.hornecker}@strath.ac.uk

Abstract. We present a study that explores people's affective responses when experiencing data represented through different modalities. In particular, we are interested in investigating how data representations that address haptic/tactile and sonic perception are experienced. We describe the creation of a number of data-driven artifacts that all represent the same dataset. In taking a phenomenological approach to our analysis, we used the Repertory Grid Technique (RGT) during a group session to elicit participant's personal constructs, which are used to describe and compare these artifacts. Our analysis examines these, traces the emergence of one exemplary personal construct and highlights other emergent themes. Our findings consist of a number of elicited constructs that illuminate how the affective qualities of data driven artifacts relate to the type of modality in use.

Keywords: Data Representation, Modality, Phenomenology, Repertory Grid Technique, User-Experience.

1   Introduction

In contemporary society, data representations are an important and essential part of many aspects of our daily lives. Representations in the form of demographic statistics, financial reports, environmental data, economic trends and others are being widely distributed by the media, which compete for people's attention and comprehension. The vast majority of these use the visual modality to represent the data, requiring the reader to interpret and gain meaning from the data using only their visual sense.

In our research we examine the user experience, and in particular, the affective responses to data represented using a range of modalities. Our work is motivated by recent literature that emphasizes the felt experience of interaction [1], as well as the re-emergence of phenomenology within the HCI community, as an approach to better understand peoples' experience of technology (cf. [2]). Phenomenology, from a philosophical perspective, is concerned with people's lived experience of the phenomena that is being researched. From a methodological perspective, it demands a process that emphasizes the unique subjective experiences of research participants. Don Ihde eloquently defines it as an investigation into "the conditions of what makes things appear as such" [3]. In the context of our research we take a phenomenological

C. Magnusson, D. Szymczak, and S. Brewster (Eds.): HAID 2012, LNCS 7468, pp. 141–151, 2012.

approach to capturing the first-hand experience of participants' engagement with data-driven artifacts.

Our research is inspired by the emergence of data visualisation subfields that include: Information Aesthetics [4], Artistic Visualization [5], Data Art [6] and Casual Visualization [7]. It is based on the assumption that representing identical datasets through different modalities may support a different user experience and affective response. In particular, we are interested in investigating how representations that address haptic/tactile and sonic perception are experienced, and in exploring the particular strengths of these modalities [8]. By representing the data through haptic and auditory feedback we anticipated that this would offer an opportunity to gain insight into people's experience of feeling and listening to data, in contrast to simply viewing data representations.

We here present an explorative user study conducted as part of this larger research agenda. Three data representations were developed, each focusing on different perceptual modalities. We ran a focus group based on the Repertory Grid Technique [9] to assess participants experience and responses to the three data-driven artifacts. We used an inductive and grounded approach for analysing the outcome of the RGT study (participants comparison of the representations along self-chosen categories) as well as the process of the session.

2   Data Artifacts

As a first step, we selected a data source to be represented. The main criteria was that it must be socially relevant and from a trustworthy source. A number of datasets were identified that included economic, environmental, demographic and geographical data. From these we selected a dataset that represents the latest global urban outdoor air pollution figures from almost 1100 cities in 91 countries. For our study, the annual mean PM10 ug/m^3 for six countries (Greece: 44, Ireland: 15, India: 109, Egypt: 138, United Kingdom: 23 and Turkey: 66) was used and all the data-driven artifacts produced represented this same dataset [10].

Our RGT study utilizes the 'triad' technique, which involves participants identifying a quality dimension of three given objects, such that two of the objects are similar in some way and the third is relatively dissimilar [9]. For this reason, three modalities were identified and an artifact was produced for each. These are: SonicData (auditory modality), DataBox (cross-modal (haptic and auditory)) and a Bar Graph (visual modality). Besides using different representational modalities, two of the artifacts (DataBox and SonicData) require active manipulation to elicit information, whereas the Bar Graph only requires the participants to look at it. Also, SonicData and the Bar Graph both use a single modality to represent the data, with SonicData utilizing an alternative modality to the 'standard' visual modality. DataBox is defined as employing cross-modal output. Cross-modal output, in the context of this research, uses more than one modality to represent the same data. Its use of the different senses allows the characteristics of one sensory modality to be transformed into stimuli for another sensory modality [11].

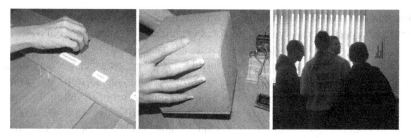

Fig. 1. Data-driven artefacts. Left: *SonicData*, Middle: *DataBox*, Right: Bar Graph.

SonicData: is a bespoke device that represents the dataset by playing sonic tones at certain frequencies through a tactile interface. Users of *SonicData* are presented with a labelled surface and a small coloured wooden cube. Placing the cube over each label plays a tone in a frequency representing the urban air pollution of this country. The tones' frequency is mapped to the level of air pollution; high pollution results in a high frequency sound and low pollution will result in a low sound, e.g. 1380 Hertz (Egypt) and 150 Hertz (Ireland). *DataBox:* is a wireless cube device ($10cm^3$) created for this study, which represents the dataset through haptic and auditory feedback. The six faces of the cube represent the six countries of the dataset. When the user hovers each face over a scanning station, an LCD display located within this station shows the name of the selected country. *DataBox* immediately responds by knocking on the internal walls. The rate of knocks corresponds to the level of air pollution, e.g. 15 times per minute (Ireland) and 138 times per minute (Egypt). *DataBox* consists of a microcontroller and 12-volt solenoid housed inside a hollow wooden box, and has RFID tags on the inside of each face. When hovering the box over a RFID reader it reads the closest tag, sends a message to the LCD, and wirelessly transmits a message to the microcontroller that controls the knocking. *Bar Graph|:* This representation utilized a common and recognisable format. The graph (42cm x 21cm) was labelled with the names of the six countries on the x-axis and the data was represented using solid black bars on the y-axis. We were conscious that including such a recognisable format may influence the participants responses, especially considering the unique nature of the other artifacts. However, the rationale for including such a standard format was to remind the participants that they were interacting with artifacts that serve the purpose of representing raw datasets.

3   Study Methodology

Early on, the RGT method was identified as a useful tool for dealing with user-experience and affective evaluation [12]. Although its use within the HCI research community peaked in the early eighties (for a historical overview, see [12]), recently we have seen a resurgence of interest in this technique [13, 14, 15]. It was initially developed as a clinical psychological method to empirically elicit and evaluate people's subjective experiences and meaning structures [16], and methodologically extends George Kelly's Personal Construct Theory (PCT). PCT is based on the assumption that human beings shape their understanding and meaning of the world by drawing upon past interactions and personal experiences. It states that our view of the objects, people and events we interact with is made up of a collection of bipolar dimensions, referred to as a personal construct [16]. For instance, we may judge an event in our lives as being *happy—sad, uplifting—boring, memorable—forgetful* and so on. Therefore a personal construct is a bipolar dimension of meaning for a person allowing them to compare two or more elements. Kelly suggested the RGT as a method to systematically elicit these personal constructs. In a traditional application of the RGT the researcher presents participants with elements in groups of three. Once they have become familiar with the elements they must identify where two of the elements are similar (Convergent pole) but dissimilar from the third element (Divergent pole). What emerges is a bipolar dimension (*personal construct*). Using this bipolar dimension, the participant is asked to rate all the elements on a 5-7 scale (1: Convergent pole, 7: Divergent pole). Due to its flexibility, the RGT has been used in a wide range of fields from clinical psychology to architecture. The RGT has also been proven to be a valuable technique in phenomenological studies to understanding user experience and for understanding the perceived qualities of computational objects [2, 17]. One of the main reasons why the RGT is useful for this purpose, is that it provides an established method for eliciting user's personal constructs, in distinction to other methods such as *semantic differential*, which is usually based on predefined, given constructs [18].

The vast majority of published research that has used the RGT method was conducted by individually interviewing a number of participants (normally 8-15) for 1-2 hours each [9]. The approach taken for our study differs by eliciting personal constructs from participants during an open group discussion, which would later be transcribed and analysed. The effort involved for both participants and researcher in individual interviews is one of the main known disadvantages of the RGT [12], and a group study reduces the cognitive workload for all involved. On the other hand, there are well-known problems with group discussions, such as peer influence and smaller sample size. However, we believed that in this particular case, this approach would allow us to observe participants discussing amongst each other in a natural situation where expressing their thoughts would be part of natural social interaction.

The participants were all final-year digital media students and members of the same class and already accustomed to discussing topics in front of one another during group critiques. 15 individuals (11 male, 4 female) participated in the study, with a mean age of 22 years (Min = 19, Max = 24). It was a conscious decision to involve a group of participants who know each other well and would feel comfortable discussing their personal experiences in front of the group. The study entailed, firstly, dividing the group into three subgroups. The subgroups then had 15 minutes to engage with each of the data artifacts (45 minutes in total). This was followed by a group discussion, which involved all subgroups and was facilitated by a researcher. The entire study took place in a large room and was recorded using three video cameras directed at each artifact and three digital audio recorders positioned alongside each artifact. Subsequently transcripts were produced from audio files recorded during the familiarisation sessions.

3.1   Procedure

As this study adapted the RGT, the following sections briefly describe the steps followed during a typical RGT study, and then highlights the variations to these while conducting our study. For the purposes of this study, three artifacts were pre-selected and created by the researchers, providing the 'elements' (RGT terminology) to be examined. Participants are made familiar with the elements before the phase of construct elicitation begins. An RGT study would normally conclude by having the participants rate each of the elements on a 5-7 scale for each construct. Our study did not include this stage, as the main objective was to reveal the emergence of these constructs through an inductive approach to the analysis.

Element Familiarization: This stage allows for the participants to become familiar with the elements used in the study. The researcher typically introduces each participant to the elements and allows some time to interact with these. Generally this study stage is quite informal and not treated as of critical importance. However, for the study presented here this stage was central. Following a short introduction to the three data artifacts by the researcher, all participants were allowed 45 minutes to interact with them. The participants were not required to complete a specific task during this session but encouraged to explore and interact with all the artifacts, if at any stage they required assistance a researcher was in place to help them out. The participants were divided into groups of four, spending fifteen minutes interacting with each data artifact before moving on to the next in a round-robin pattern. All groups were encouraged to openly discuss their perception and experience as well as discussing the pertinent qualities of the artifacts with each other.

Fig. 2. Group session to elicit personal constructs from individuals

Construct Elicitation: During this stage, participants are normally interviewed individually to elicit personal constructs. Instead, for our study a group discussion was conducted (fig. 2.) and mediated by the researcher. The method used was the minimum-context triad form of construct elicitation. From a triad of elements the participants are asked to describe how two elements are similar (Convergent pole) but differ from the third (Divergent pole) [9]. This dimension is the personal construct.

The session commenced by asking participants to write down as many personal constructs as they could think of. After a few minutes they were asked to explain their constructs aloud and the group openly discussed each of these. This discussion also generated further new constructs. These were elicited by the researcher 'laddering' the discussion by asking participants 'why' certain constructs are important to them. Constructs were only recorded if the majority of the participants agreed. This process was repeated until participants could no longer think of meaningful distinctions or similarities among the triad of artifacts.

4   Findings

Our analysis went through four steps, from filtering and collapsing the elicited constructs, over classifying them as ergonomic or experience-oriented (hedonic) to tracing their emergence and finally highlighting major themes exposed during the study.

Filtering: In total 35 sets of bi-polar constructs were elicited during the group discussion session. For this analysis, the list was shortened to 27 constructs by collapsing those that were semantically related into one construct. For example we collapsed the constructs Novel and Innovative into the one construct (Novel).

Table 1. Personal constructs (Hedonic Quality) elicited during the RGT study, the arrows for each artifacts points to the pole of the dimension. A: DataBox, B: SonicData , C: BarGraph.

		DataBox	SonicData	BarGraph	
PC1	Novel	⇐	⇐	⇒	Familiar
PC2	Experimental	⇐	⇐	⇒	Traditional
PC3	Instinctual	⇐	⇐	⇒	Cerebral
PC4	Fun, Stimulating	⇐	⇐	⇒	Dull, Boring
PC5	Warm	⇐	⇐	⇒	Cold
PC6	Colourful	⇐	⇐	⇒	Black & White
PC7	Playful	⇐	⇐	⇒	Task-orientated
PC8	Immersive	⇐	⇐	⇒	Non-immersive
PC9	Sonic	⇐	⇐	⇒	Silent
PC10	Sophisticated	⇐	⇐	⇒	Non- Sophisticated
PC11	Intensive	⇐	⇒	⇒	Subtle
PC12	Strong	⇐	⇒	⇒	Weak
PC13	Artificial	⇐	⇒	⇒	Organic

Classification: As the objective of the study was to examine the users' affective responses, we focused the analysis on constructs that demonstrate affective or hedonic qualities (cf. [19]) rather than ergonomic qualities (task-orientated and related to traditional usability principles such as efficiency). Hedonic quality (HQ) comprises quality dimensions with no obvious relation to tasks, such as novelty, innovativeness, attractiveness etc [19]. From the list of 26 sets of constructs, 13 were classified as HQ by two researchers (Table 1). Table 1 illustrates the elicited (HQ) personal constructs (PC1-13) It shows, for instance, that the group characterized both *DataBox* and *SonicData* as 'Novel' but unlike the Bar Graph which was characterized as being 'Familiar' (PC1). They also agreed that *SonicData* and the Bar Graph should be described as 'Organic' whereas *DataBox* was 'Artificial' (PC13).

Tracing: The objective át this stage was to trace the emergence of the hedonic constructs in order to better understand the meaning associated with these constructs. This was achieved by examining the transcribed familiarization and group session as well as field notes taking during and after the study. It is important to note that as part of this study these field notes were an integral element and were already "a step toward data analysis" [20]. For reasons of brevity the exemplar construct that we have chosen to trace here is PC3 *{Instinctual—Cerebral}*.

Table 1 shows that the group agreed that *DataBox* and *SonicData* should be described as *Instinctual* whereas the Bar Graph was described as *Cerebral*. This reliance on instinct was evident during the Familiarisation Session. While interacting with the *DataBox* and *SonicData,* the participants were continuously seeking real-world analogies for further insight into the artifacts. On numerous occasions, participants in all four familiarisation sub-groups compared the output from *DataBox* to the characteristics of living beings. P3: *"It's like a heartbeat"*, P2: *"It feels like it is dying"*, P5: *"India is dead"*. P7 also remarked that the knocking on the box could be compared to *"the pumping of our lungs and the beating of our heart"*. The participants also used real-world analogies while using *SonicData*, however, these tended to be more artificial in nature, for instance in this discussion segment: P3: *"Greece sounds like a dialling tone."* P3: *"The UK is kind of nice, it sounds like a small ship."* P5 *"Yeah, like a sonar".* P2 *"No, it sounds like you are dialling a phone."* P1: *"Then the high-pitched ones are the highest ones".*

During the Construct Elicitation session the group explained this personal construct further by describing the graph as a thing that you have to learn to use. They explained how they have been taught to use bar graphs throughout their education and they see them merely as tools; one remarked *"You can tell instantly which is the worst of which is the best - there is no confusion, you do not have to look any further".* The mapping used in the other artifacts, however, were new to the participants. They spoke about not having any prior training in the use of these and having to rely on their instinct to understand what the output represented.

Themes. *{Linguistic}* An interesting theme that emerged from the study was that the language used by participants while interacting with the *DataBox* and *SonicData* was, in general, more emotive than with the Bar Graph. There was frequent use of expressive descriptions such as: annoying, hurts, beautiful, healthy, alarming, relaxing, dead, urgent, fun, torture, irritating and intense; used in relation to the *DataBox* and *SonicData* that was not evident in the conversations about the Bar Graph. *{Consequences verses Implications}* It was also found that the three sub-groups discussions of the Bar Graph during the familiarisation session generally related to discussing and speculating about the causes of pollution, whereas discussions around the other artifacts generally related to the effect that poor pollution has on the inhabitants of the countries. This is highlighted in the following extract from the familiarization session: [Bar Graph] *P1 ...It looks like poorer countries have more pollution than richer countries. P2 yes P3 but why is Egypt more polluted than India? P2 but isn't India poorer P3 that has got nothing to do with the air? P2 but generally poor countries are more polluted as they have so many people there...*

[*SonicData*] *P3: "... the sound of each is so annoying" P4: "imagine living in Egypt, it would be pretty annoying to have such pollution also" P5: "as well as India". P5: "Greece is by far my most favorite one" P2: "No, mine is the United Kingdom"....*

[*DataBox*] *P2: "... that could be healthy Ireland?" P1: "Healthy Ireland! No, cause if my heart was beating that slow I would be almost dead." P3: "Yes, but what we are feeling at the moment is Egypt." P2: "Yeah, but that feels healthy." P3: "Yeah, that sounds good, it sounds like progress, it sounds like it's going well..."*

{The Felt Dimension} Another theme to emerge was the participants' way of phrasing how they experienced and interpreted the data artifacts. When using the *DataBox* they talked about 'feeling' the data and associated it with a human-heartbeat. On occasions when the frequency of knocks decreased, the participant holding the *DataBox* remarked that they felt the country was 'dying'. Affective responses were also evident with *SonicData*. Participants described some of the sounds as being 'annoying' or 'painful' and equated unpleasant sounds with increased pollution.

{Rating} Also, in relation to *SonicData*, the participants spoke about which sound was their favorite, and used this as an attempt to map the least and most polluted countries. The following exchange exemplifies this: **P1:** "I like that one the best [Greece]." **P2:** "I like that one [UK]." **P1:** "What's next, Turkey, India and Egypt." **P3:** "Think about it though, what is the nicest to listen to?" **P5:** "Greece is nice." **P3:** "I like the UK." **P2:** "The lower ones are nice so the pollution must be low." **P1:** "Yes, I like the lower ones." **P5:** "My favorite's Greece."

These behaviors may be interpreted as the participants' affectively responding to the *DataBox* and *SonicData* in a manner that was not evident with the Bar Graph. While we did expect the responses from the *DataBox* and *SonicData* to be more extreme than the Bar Graph, given this format does not leave much space for interpretation, the acute difference in the style of language used by the participants to describe their experience was noticeable and somewhat unexpected. The affective response to *DataBox* and *SonicData* is furthermore reflected in Table 1, where participants tended to associate these more often with what could be considered the more emotional and fun-related pole of a construct (e.g. primal, fun, warm, playful, immersive). Interestingly, *SonicData* was considered artificial (and not organic).

Other Observations. During the familiarisation session we observed a distinct difference in how the three sub-groups situated themselves and moved around the artifacts. While interacting with *DataBox* and *SonicData* the members of a group were continuously switching positions in order to interact with the artifacts but also to observe others interacting with the artifacts. This was not evident with any group at the Bar Graph. In this case, all members of a group stood motionless in front of the graph until they were asked to move to another artifact. We also noted that when a member of the group talked about *DataBox* and *SonicData* that the other members sought to maintain eye contact throughout the discussion. This could be described as an attempt to discover more about what others were saying and feeling as they used the artifacts. Conversely, when the groups were viewing the Bar Graph they tended to consistently look at the graph, even when other members were speaking. In this case, the choice of representation might contribute to this behaviour pattern – the Bar Graph representation has an orientation, and even if it would be on a piece of paper on the table, it would not be as easy for the group to surround it as this was for the other two data artifacts.

While there is evidence which supports the case that representing data using non-visual artifacts evokes more affective responses, we also observed that the participants had some difficulty mapping the data to the artifact output, for example whether frequent knocking (*DataBox*) represented a high or low rate of pollution. In the early stages of the session participants spent some time discussing this issue. However, once consensus was met, the conversation soon switched to issues related to the source of the dataset. In the future we would consider supplying a legend with the non-traditional data representations in order to allow the users to concentrate on the artifact as opposed to the mapping.

5   Conclusion and Discussion

This paper presented a study that investigated users' affective responses when experiencing data represented through different types and levels of modalities. We explored this by conducting an adapted RGT group study using three data-driven artifacts. During a group session with 15 participants, 35 personal constructs were elicited. For the purpose of analysis this list was shortened to 13 that demonstrated a hedonic quality. It is clear from this list that the participants perceived *DataBox* and *SonicData* as being more similar than the Bar Graph. Apart from the obvious novel characteristics of these artifacts over the familiar format of the Bar Graph, we also believe that the interactive quality of these artifacts influenced the participants to see them as more alike.

We do however recognise some limitations with this study. Primarily, the differences in the artifacts may have caused some difficulties when comparing them, specifically in regards to the temporal nature of the mapping. In both *DataBox* and *SonicData* the mapping is distributed over time and thus not simultaneously perceivable whereas the Bargraph allows for concurrent perception.

In the analysis we chose one personal construct *[Instinctual—Cerebral]* and traced its emergence using field notes and transcriptions from the group session. This analysis reveals that the participants relied heavily on instinct, previous experiences and real-world analogies to infer data insight and meaning from both *DataBox* and *SonicData*. Conversely, the participants found that the Bar Graph is a tool they have been trained to use over a long period and thus did not engage them emotionally. They tended to have more abstract, causality-oriented discussions about the content of the Bar Graph, whereas they were more concerned about what the data represented by the *DataBox* and *SonicData* would mean for people's lives, and used more emotive language to describe the data.

Our experience has shown that, given a group that is comfortable discussing with each other, a group approach towards RGT construct elicitation can be useful, in particular in allowing us to trace the emergence of constructs from participants' direct initial responses to the elements. We intend to further validate this methodological adaption by conducting a series of group and individual studies using the same set of elements. Although the findings require further investigation and analysis, in particular we intend to trace the emergence of further constructs, we believe that we have shown evidence that the modality and modality combinations used to represent data do influence the users' experience and affective responses.

References

1. McCarthy, J., Wright, P.: Technology as Experience. The MIT Press (2004)
2. Fallman, D.: Romance with the Materials of Mobile Interaction: A Phenomenological Approach to the Design of Mobile Information Technology. Doctoral Thesis. Larsson & Co's Tryckeri, Umea University, Sweden (2003)
3. Ihde, D.: If Phenomenology Is an Albatross, Is Post-phenomenology Possible? In: Ihde, D., Selinger, E. (eds.) Chasing Technoscience: Matrix for Materiality. Indiana University Press, Indianapolis (2003)
4. Lau, A., Vande Moere, A.: Towards a Model of Information Aesthetics in Information Visualization. In: Proc. of the Int. Conference Information Visualization, pp. 87–92. IEEE (2007)
5. Viégas, F.B., Wattenberg, M.: Artistic Data Visualization: Beyond Visual Analytics. In: Schuler, D. (ed.) HCII 2007 and OCSC 2007. LNCS, vol. 4564, pp. 182–191. Springer, Heidelberg (2007)
6. Manovich, L.: Data Visualization as New Abstraction and as Anti-Sublime. In: Hawk, B., Reider, D., Oviedo, O. (eds.) Small Tech: The Culture of Digital Tools, Electronic Mediations, vol. 22. University of Minnesota, Minneapolis (2008)
7. Pousman, Z., Stasko, J.T., Mateas, M.: Casual Information Visualization: Depictions of Data in Everyday Life. IEEE Transactions on Visualization and Computer Graphics, 1145–1152 (2007)
8. Hornecker, E.: Let's Get Physical: The Role of Physicality in Tangible and Embodied Interactions. ACM Interactions Magazine 18(2), 19–23 (March/April)
9. Fransella, F., Bannister, D., Bell, R.: A Manual for Repertory Grid Technique. Wiley-Blackwell (2003)
10. The Guardian, http://www.guardian.co.uk/environment/datablog/2011/sep/26/global-air-pollution-who?CMP=twt_fd (accessed: November 15, 2011)
11. Lenay, C., Canu, S., Villon, P.: Technology and Perception; the Contribution of Sensory Substitution Systems. In: Proc. of Cognitive Technology, pp. 44–53. IEEE (1997)
12. Fallman, D., Waterworth, J.A.: Capturing User Experiences of Mobile Information Technology with the Repertory Grid Technique. J. Human Technology 6(2), 250–268 (2010)

13. Grill, T., Flexer, A., Cunningham, S.: Identification of Perceptual Qualities in Textural Sounds using the Repertory Grid Methodology. In: Proc. of AM 2011. ACM (2011)
14. Cunningham, S.: Applying personal construct psychology in sound design using a repertory grid. In: Proc. of the 5th Audio Mostly Conference AM 2010, pp. 1–6. ACM, N.Y. (2010)
15. Edwards, H.M., McDonald, S., Young, S.M.: Choosing field methods: a reflection on a RepGrid study. In: Proc. of NordiCHI 2010, pp. 639–642. ACM (2010)
16. Kelly, G.A.: The psychology of personal constructs, Norton, New York (1955)
17. Introna, L.D., Whittaker, L.: The phenomenology of information systems evaluation: overcoming the subject/object dualism. In: Proc. of Working Conference on Global and Organizational Discourse about Information Technology, pp. 155–175 (2002)
18. Gable, R.K., Wolf, M.B.: Instrument development in the affective domain, 2nd edn. Kluwer Academic Publishers, Boston (1993)
19. Hassenzahl, M., Platz, A., Burmester, M., Lehner, K.: Hedonic and ergonomic quality aspects determine a software's appeal. In: Proc. of CHI 2000, pp. 201–208. ACM, NY (2000)
20. Morgan, D.L.: Focus groups as qualitative research. Sage, London (1988)

Author Index